The Boston Bruins gratefully acknowledge the support of the following organizations in celebrating the team's 75th Anniversary.

By Clark Booth

Photo Editor Steve Babineau

TEHABI BOOKS
DEL MAR, CALIFORNIA

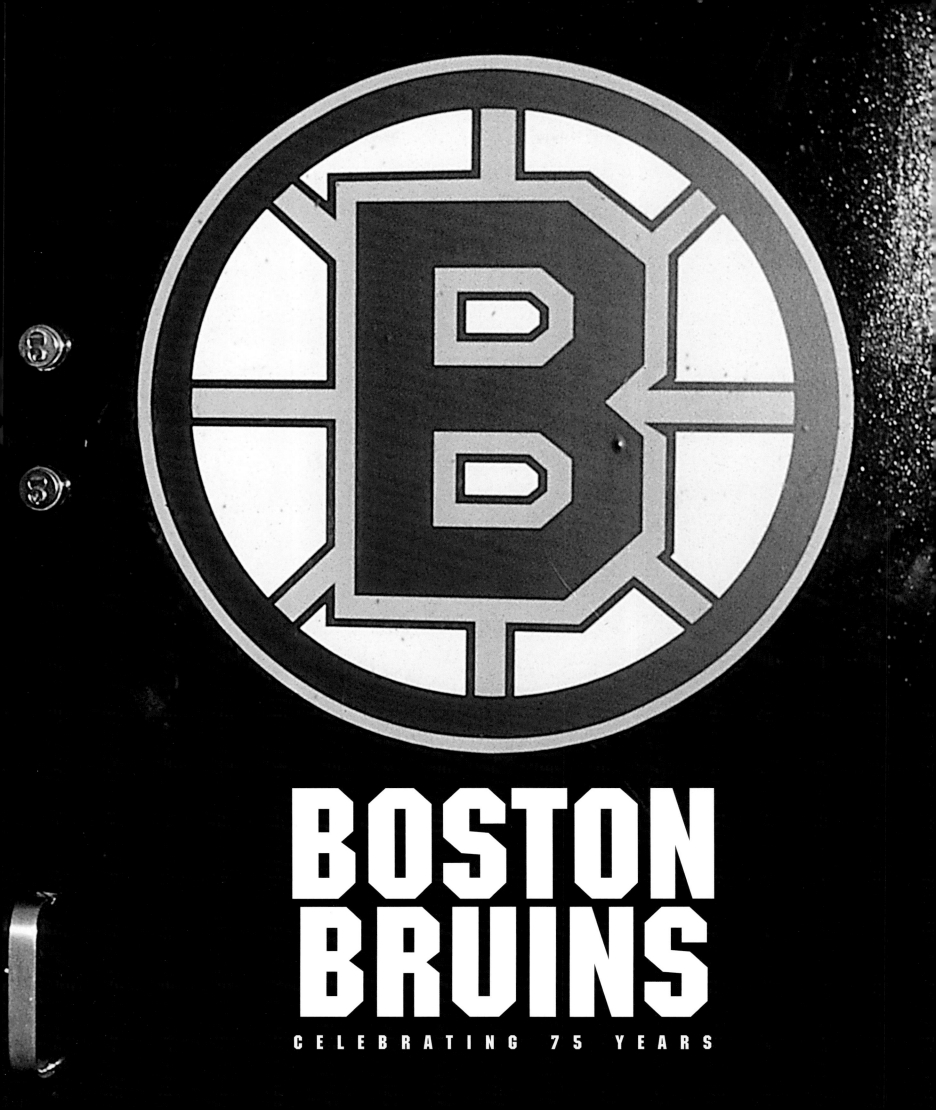

BOSTON BRUINS

CELEBRATING 75 YEARS

Acknowledgments from the author

Russ and Trudie Booth courted at Rangers games in the '30s. Anne and Clark favored Sunday nights with the Leafs in the '60s. Tracy and Guy were regulars in Section 92 while Scott and Carolyn had the Bruins for an early date in the '80s. As young lads in the '70s, Matthew and Scott cavorted on the darkened Garden ice surface while Dad did his interviews. In the '90s, lovely Alyssa was 13 months old when she debuted at the Bruins' annual charity festival. This book salutes all of that. Special thanks to Nate Greenberg for making it happen.

Photo captions:

pages 2–3:
Exaggerated imagery captures the dash, verve, and power of Cam Neely.

page 8:
The Bruins' Lochinvar. Misfortune only deepened Bobby Orr's mystique.

page 9:
Harvard has served as a Bruins training ground. Ted Donato is the latest example.

pages 10–11:
In a definitive moment, Bruins' Jonathan, O'Reilly, and Wensink rumble with the Canadiens, May 1978.

page 12:
Policing his turf, Kyle McLaren does what comes naturally for a Bruins defenseman.

page 13:
Seventy-five years of history affirm the Montreal Canadiens as the Bruins' favorite foe.

page 14:
In the winter of '97–'98, Russian teenager Sergei Samsonov became the Bruins' latest star.

page 15:
Bruins history crested with John Bucyk's victory lap, May 1970.

TEHABI BOOKS, which designed and produced *Boston Bruins: Celebrating 75 Years*, has conceived and produced many award-winning, visually oriented books. "Tehabi," which symbolizes the spirit of teamwork, derives its name from the Hopi Indian tribe of the southwestern United States. Tehabi Books is located in Del Mar, California.

Chris Capen—*President*; Tom Lewis—*Editorial and Design Director*; Sharon Lewis—*Controller*; Nancy Cash—*Managing Editor*; Andy Lewis—*Art Director*; Sarah Morgans—*Editorial Assistant*; Sam Lewis—*Webmaster*; Ross Eberman—*Director of Corporate Sales*; Tim Connolly—*Sales and Marketing Manager*.

Additional support for *Boston Bruins: Celebrating 75 Years* was provided by Steve Babineau—*Photo Editor*; Jeff Campbell—*Copy Editor*; Gail Fink—*Copy Proofer*; Ken DellaPenta—*Indexer*.

www.tehabi.com

Photography credits appear on page 180.

Library of Congress Cataloging-in-Publication Data

Booth, Clark, 1939–
    Boston Bruins: celebrating 75 years / by Clark Booth.
        p.   cm.
      ISBN: 07607-1126-7 (paperback) — ISBN: 07607-1127-5 (hardcover) — ISBN: 1-887656-11-1 (leatherbound).
    1. Boston Bruins (Hockey team)—History. 2. Boston Bruins (Hockey team)—History—pictorial works. I. Title.
GV848.B6B66 1998
796.962´64´0974461—dc21
                                                      98-24815
                                                      CIP

98 99 00 01 02 / TB 10 9 8 7 6 5 4 3 2 1

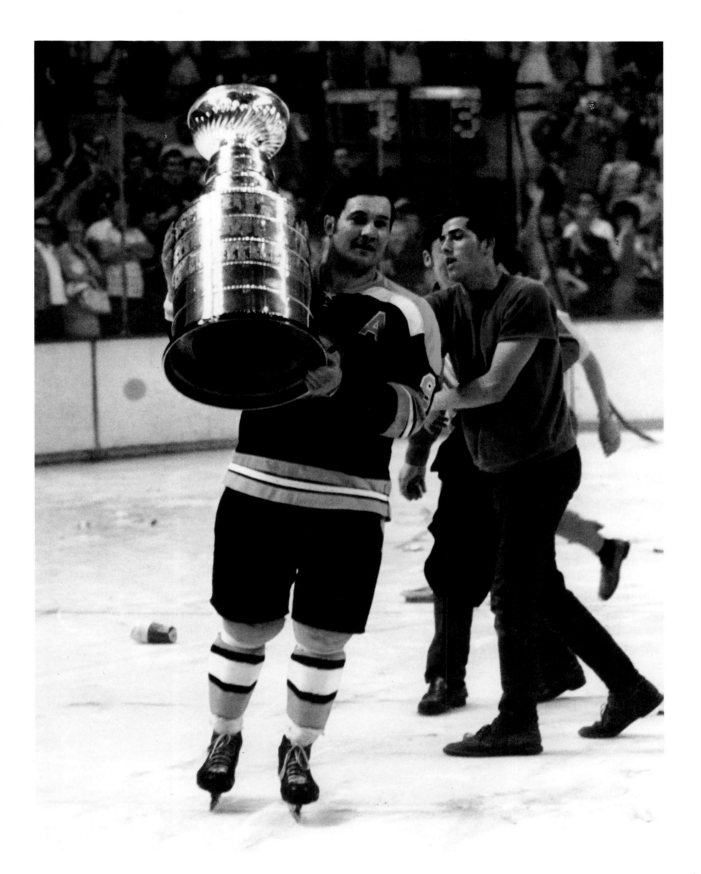

WE ARE THE BRUINS

CHAPTER ONE

There have been more successful teams, if you measure success in wins, losses, and titles. But none has had a history more rowdy and bold. If the Bruins story was a tale done by Shakespeare, it would have been a sequel to his loving portraits of the Lancastrian kings, whose recklessness was at the core of their charm and whose excesses were invariably redeemed by valor. There have been Bruins teams who believed that a loss of honor, however slight, is too high a price to pay for a mere victory, nor would their zealous followers have it any other way.

Moments that vividly illustrate the Bruins spirit are plentiful. But none surpass the rollicking ride to the Cup in the spring of 1970 when "the Big Bad Bruins," as they were pleased to be known, ran roughshod over the entire game, laughing all the way. It was a great team, enormously talented and hellacious both on and off the ice. But their best quality was their comradeship. This was a true band of brothers. The frozen ponds of the National Hockey League composed their Agincourt. And if Bobby Orr was their Prince Hal, the Falstaffian role—albeit with lots more gumption on the battlefield—was played splendidly by Gerry Cheevers. Other great teams have had as much power, skill, and fire. But none have had more kinship.

Nearly three decades later the memory is still warm, not merely of the lusty triumphs, but of the sheer joy

"Obladi obla-da, Life goes on, Bra-lala, How the life goes on."

those Bruins derived from being young, gifted, and—they clearly believed—destined. Late in the season, as they realized they were going to roll to the Cup, the merriment in the locker room was fabulous, and at odd moments, usually after practice, they would sing. A Beatles tune that was then new, "Ob-la-di, Ob-la-da," became their anthem of sorts.

It would always begin with Cheevers. He would pipe up out of the blue, while stripping himself of his equipment: "Desmond has a barrow in the market place, Molly is the singer in a band."

Then other players would roll in easily; "Desmond says to Molly, Girl I like your face, And Molly says this as she takes him by the hand."

And by the time they reached the chorus, most of the team would be singing, "Obladi oblada, Life goes on, Bra-lala, How the life goes on."

Mind you, this was a tough team. There were no college boys, and most lacked even a high-school degree. They'd been struggling up the hockey ladder since they were 14, and they could romp through the alehouses of Eastcheap as giddily as they pounded through the league. There wasn't a one of them who had not come up the hard way. "You're never a Saturday hero in this game," Harry Sinden, their then boyish coach, has said. "Hockey players have to slug their way to the top, like fighters did in the old days. You have to go to the corner gym and learn your trade." And that's where every one of them had sprung from, the corner gyms scattered all over the vast, cold, lonely landscape of the game of hockey, which is why the music that came from them at the end of their long, hard trek seemed particularly touching. I've been present at many championship occasions. But I only saw one other team celebrate its triumph with song: the 1979 Pittsburgh Pirates who, under the spell of the equally Falstaffian Willie Stargell, punctuated their improbable World Series victory over the Baltimore Orioles with rousing renditions of "We Are Family!" That tune had not yet been written in 1970, but it was what these Bruins were singing as well.

Their St. Crispin's Day was May 10, 1970. It was also Mother's Day, and the old Garden, brimming with at least three thousand more people than the fire laws allowed, was a sauna. The overmatched but stubborn St. Louis Blues had pushed them into overtime without greatly altering the certainty of the outcome. Only 40 seconds from the start of sudden death, a swooping Bobby Orr took a perfect feed from Derek Sanderson and

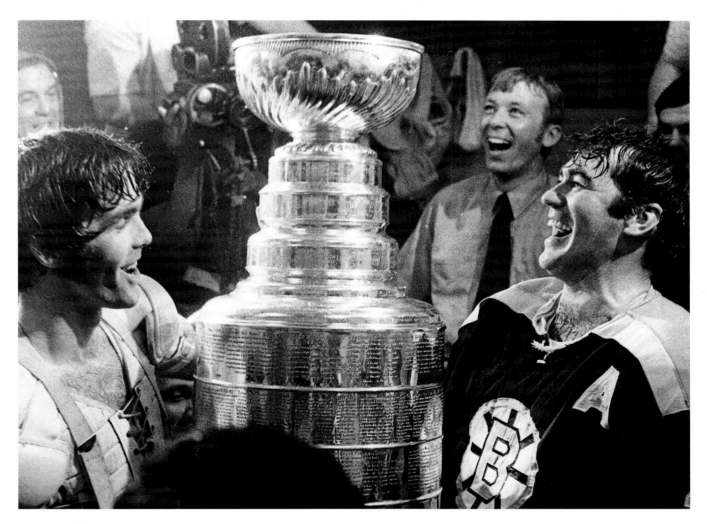

A brief mellow moment on Mother's Day, 1970, finds the rowdy Derek Sanderson (left) and his cerebral linemate Eddie Westfall basking in the glow of the Cup. Also reveling in the scene is the author (rear), then a young reporter not yet wise enough to remain a bit detached from the story. Later, after the flowing of much wine, Lord Stanley's priceless silver bowl got tossed around the Bruins' quarters like a volleyball. It was a helluva party. His Grace must have been rolling around in his grave.

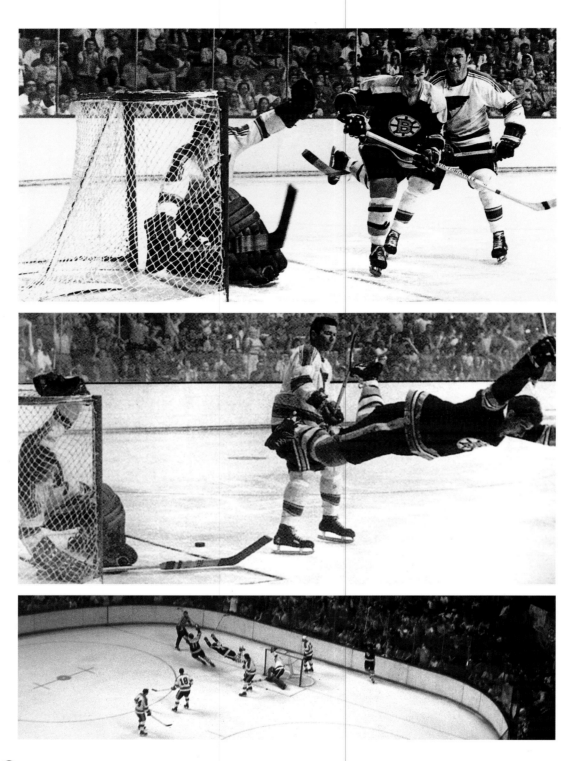

Orr's epic moment was caught for all time in these dramatic images. Ray Lussier's shot is center. Ray, a photographer who was not a regular on the beat, didn't have a pass, and arrived at the game late. Nor did Ray believe it was the best picture he took that day. But Sam Cohen, a sports editor right out of central casting, knew better. "Print it and print it BIG!" said Sam. When Ray protested he had better shots, Cohen snarled, "Print that . . . picture." So they did, to the everlasting fame of both Orr and Ray Lussier.

stuffed the puck past the Blues' legendary goalie Glenn Hall. It remains a split second of sporting history that's frozen in time thanks in part to the photograph of the late Ray Lussier of the long-defunct Boston tabloid, the RECORD-AMERICAN. Lussier caught it perfectly. There is Hall staggering almost drunkenly in the crease, the puck rebounding from the goal, as the crowd soars. Noel Picard, the petulant Blues defenseman beaten on the play, is scowling. He has punctuated Orr's heroics with a spiteful trip with his stick. Which is why Orr, bursting with joy, is soaring through the air as if on eagle's wings. It is the most famous photo in the history of hockey.

The celebration that followed was epic. For better or worse—opinions are mixed—no team ever partied harder than the Big Bad Bruins. The jubilant ceremonies on the ice, with the skating of the Stanley Cup in scores of victory laps, was but the warm-up for a festival in the locker room that lasted five hours and then moved onto the streets, threading through various downtown bistros until noon the next day when the entire team, greatly the worse for wear, gathered on the mayor's balcony at City Hall to be trumpeted by some one hundred thousand screaming admirers. There, a part-time rodeo bronco buster and full-time right winger named Johnny McKenzie, known as "Pie," topped the proceedings by dumping a bucket of beer over the head of Mayor Kevin White. It was Homeric.

But in all of the revelry, which was the most genuinely joyous I ever saw in sports, the highlight for me was something small and mellow. Deep into the wild locker room scene, awash in champagne, Cheevers suddenly broke

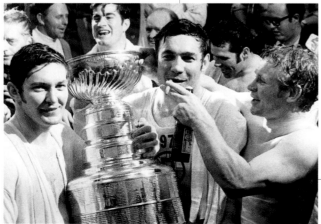

Only irascible Johnny McKenzie (right) would mess with John "the Chief" Bucyk's trademark cigar. Meanwhile, Fred Stanfield (left) mugs with the Cup. They formed a great "second" line. Exulting behind them is preppy owner Westie Adams, then only 25, a fact we never let him forget.

into the song, and this time they all joined quickly: "Happy ever after in the market place, Desmond lets the children lend a hand. Molly stays at home and does her pretty face, And in the evening she still sings it with the band." While the place was jammed with interlopers, heavyweights of media, politicians, and celebrities who hadn't always been around, there was a hush. You didn't have to know them well to understand that this was not just celebration but ritual. "Obladi oblada, Life goes on, Bra-lala, How the life goes on." The whimsy of the tune didn't register with me at the time. Being more a student of Dvorák than Lennon, I didn't pick up on its subtle hint of fatalistic nonchalance. Otherwise I might have found it even more poignant.

With a little luck, the Big Bad Bruins might have dominated the game for a generation, much as the Montreal Canadiens did after World War II. But their timing was bad. They came along just when hockey was being dragged into an era of monumental change featuring rampant expansion, new leagues, escalating salaries, and the liberation of players. They got caught in the transition. Four days after Orr sailed through the air and New England danced with joy, they lost their brilliant young coach, Harry Sinden.

They blew the Cup the next season, then rebounded to win it again two years later. But it wasn't quite the same, and then a raft of key "character" players, led by Cheevers, departed. The music they thought would never end was over. There followed the painful deterioration of Orr's surgically ravaged knees, until at the age of 27 he was finished. Mother's Day of 1970 was not only the high-water mark of the Orr era but of the Bruins' entire history. A generation later they still seek to reclaim that high ground. "Obladi oblada, Life goes on bra-lala, How the life goes on."

"We were a great club, and we were all kids. . . ."

—Woody Dumart

It has never been a hugely lucky franchise. In a spartan, no-excuse game in which injury and other imponderables weigh heavily for all, it is a complex claim to make. But in point of fact the premature demise of the Orr era marked the second time a potential Bruins dynasty had been thwarted by conditions beyond their control. The first victim was the superb prewar team that won the Stanley Cup in 1939 and 1941, featuring the last utterances of Eddie Shore, the artistry of Bill Cowley and Dit Clapper, and the coming of age of the fabled Kraut line of Milt Schmidt, Woody Dumart, and Bobby Bauer. Dumart, the Krauts' gifted left winger, recalls, "We were a great club and we were all kids. Frankie Brimsek was still a young goalie. We finished first four years in a row. The last time we won the Cup, we swept Detroit in the finals four straight. We hadn't even reached our peak. And then, along came the war."

Schmidt, Dumart, and Bauer were sent off to that war in a patriotic display that might make us blush today. On the night of February 10, 1942, the Bruins hosted the archrival Canadiens and thrashed them as rarely they ever did, 8–1. The Krauts—or, more precisely, "the Kitchener Kids" as they were then being called to assuage the prevailing Germanic phobia—combined for 11 points, with Bauer scoring twice and Dumart once. After the game, the two teams lined up at center ice with the Krauts between them. In a gesture that left the lads a tad breathless, the Bruins' notoriously parsimonious management presented them with checks covering the balance of their salaries for the year plus bonuses and gold aviator wristwatches. Jack Crawford, representing the team, presented them with gold "dog tags." The crowd cheered mightily.

And then something happened that those who were there would never forget. In an entirely impromptu gesture, the players—both their teammates and the much-loathed foes from Montreal—hoisted the three Kraut liners on their shoulders and collectively skated them around the rink while the lady at the organ played "Auld Lang Syne" and the crowd bellowed and wept. When the music ended the Krauts were carried off the ice, into their dressing room, and on to the Royal Canadian Air Force.

It seems something borrowed from Hollywood, but it was a very different time, only nine weeks after Pearl Harbor. The Allies were reeling in North Africa. Singapore was falling.

1995 "Last Hurrah" Jersey and Garden Seat

The Kraut line had a wonderful flair for the dramatic. In March 1952, five years after he'd prematurely retired under pressure from his family, Bobby Bauer (left) came back to play one more game with his buddies on a night honoring the three. Bobby scored a goal. So did Milt (center), the 200th of his career. Woody (right) assisted on both. When it was announced, "Goal by Schmidt, assisted by Bauer and Dumart," the crowd—the largest of the season—went berserk. By whipping the Blackhawks, 4–0, they nailed down a playoff berth. The sentiment of the evening was overpowering. And when it was over, Bobby Bauer slipped quietly back into retirement.

THE DISCOVERY OF ORR

It has been called, without so much as a hint of irreverence, "the Bethlehem of hockey." It is the small Ontario resort town of Gananoque on the St. Lawrence River, about 20 miles northeast of Kingston, a rugged and pretty place that sportsmen have long found a fine retreat for fishing and hunting. But on this occasion, in April of 1960, hockey men came to Gananoque to watch mere kids—most of them 14 and 15 years old—battle for the Bantam Division Championship of Canada. The title game pitted Scarboro against Parry Sound.

Five of the hockey men present represented the once-mighty Boston Bruins, who had landed in the NHL cellar that season, missing the playoffs for only the sixth time in their history. They'd gone six years without developing a top player. The rebuilding was way overdue. In Boston's delegation was owner Weston Adams, general manager Lynn Patrick, coach Milt Schmidt, chief scout Baldy Cotton, and Wren Blair, manager of their Kingston farm team. They had come to Gananoque to get a look at two 15-year-old prospects they owned. Long lost to history, the boys' names were Rick Eaton and Doug Higgins.

The game was but minutes old when the hockey men became captivated by an improbably stunning presence on the ice. He was a five-foot, two-inch wisp of a towhead playing defense for Parry Sound. He was so young he should still have been playing "Pee Wee" hockey instead of laboring three hundred miles from home against teenage boys much older and bigger. But while the kid, at 12, was the youngest and the smallest, he was easily—Blair would later recall—the most dominant player. "He skated rings around everyone on the ice."

Schmidt concurs. "All you needed was a single glance. He wore number five on his back, had a crew cut, and his pants were slipping down below his knees. But he simply took over the game. He had such poise. He never got flustered." While his team lost, 1–0, the kid was valorous to the last rush, playing the entire game—58 minutes on the ice, plus 2 in the penalty box, which is by definition

an unreal effort at any level. "When it was over," Schmidt recalls, "we all simply said, 'Isn't he something!'"

They were five wise, craggy hockey men who together had a century and a half of experience in the game and every reason to believe they had seen it all. Yet, here they were being bowled over by a mere waif in a bantam game played in a quonset hut in the middle of nowhere. But they knew such a prodigy would not long remain a secret. Securing the kid's rights at the then legal age of 14 would not be easy. The scheming began that night. Adams took the first step. He cheerily volunteered to "donate" one thousand bucks a year to help support the Parry Sound Bantams, which suddenly became his favorite youth program. If the Parry Sounders detected an ulterior motive in his philanthropy, they were too polite to object. But hockey people should not have been fooled.

The Adams ownership's fondness for tight fiscal policy was legend. When Weston began tossing thousand dollar bills around, alarm bells ought to have gone off all over the game. However, the next crucial step was much more complex. Financing the hometown team helped ingratiate the Bruins but it did not guarantee they'd land the boy when he came of age. They had to woo the family and convince the parents that he should become indentured to one of the Bruins Junior amateur teams when he turned 14. That and only that would lock him up.

The mission was entrusted to Wren Blair, who was a lifelong hockey grunt known as "the Bird" because of his alleged resemblance to "the Penguin," the Burgess Meredith character in the old BATMAN TV series. He was disarmingly down-to-earth in his Runyonesque way. "Wren Blair didn't get the credit he deserved, but he's the real hero of this story for the Bruins," his old friend, Harry Sinden, insists. "Wren was the guy who hung around the town for months, talked with the parents constantly, bought the kid this and that, painted his house for him, bought the father clothes. Wren was the guy who persevered." He did so for two and a half years.

When the hour finally came and the boy became eligible for Junior hockey, there was one last crisis. His mom's perfectly rational reservations about letting a 14 year old move 150 miles away to play hockey began to boil over. For two days over the 1962 Labor Day weekend, Wren negotiated with the family, easing the mom's fears, guaranteeing the boy's high-school education, securing the best living accommodations, conceding special arrangements to assuage the parents' every last concern. At the end of the talks, conducted by Blair with apparently

impressive diplomatic skill, the boy signed the form that bound him to the Bruins Junior A team in Oshawa in the Ontario Hockey Association. When he signed that form under the archaic rules then in force, he became the Bruins' property for eternity. Stan Fischler, the prolific hockey historian, has correctly noted: "With that stroke of a pen he had saved a hockey franchise."

By the time the boy was 15, he was the best player in the amateurs. By the time he was 16, he was ready for the NHL and would have moved up then had the game's child labor laws not prohibited it. When he turned 18, and at last came to Boston, he was immediately proclaimed a "messiah."

And it all began that April night

under the stars in Gananoque on the St. Lawrence when Bobby Orr was only 12 years old.

"It's funny," says Schmidt, "but I'd never been there before and I've never been back to Gananoque since we went to scout Eaton and Higgins."

Six years after he was "discovered," Orr signed a historic contract aboard Hap Emms's boat. But the crotchety Emms favored his own prodigy, Gilles Marotte, and actually pondered converting Orr into a forward. Happily for the Bruins, Hap was "retired" soon after Orr arrived.

Bobby Orr's Junior Jersey

Oshawa
GENERALS

The Philippines would be next. Roy Conacher, Eddie Wiseman, Des Smith, Frankie Brimsek, and Terry Reardon (who took a Nazi bullet in the chest in France), soon followed the Krauts. Before it was over, 16 Bruins would serve in the Allied armed forces. The 1941 champs never had the pleasure of defending their title, and when they finally reassembled, their precious edge was gone. It would take another generation to get it back. "We did have a great club," says Schmidt. "And the war did come along and kind of mess that up. But at least we can still talk about it. A lot of good guys never got that chance."

The nobility of the Kraut line is a staple of the Bruins story. So is the courage of Orr trying to skate on legs that made it painful for him to walk. Later, Cam Neely was a variation on the same theme. He might have been the finest right winger since Gordie Howe had he not blown out both a knee and a hip. They had to saw the uniform off him, before his time, as they also had to do with Gord Kluzak and Michael Thelven, both felled by knee injuries. It has been a star-crossed team. When still a teen, brilliant goaltending prospect Ian Young took a puck in the eye. After a superb rookie season, Normand Leveille was dropped by a stroke at the age of 19. You find a lot of pain in the Bruins' history. Ted Green, nicknamed "Terrible Teddie," nearly died at center ice one night, and on another night, Eddie Shore, probably the fiercest fellow ever to play the game, almost killed an opponent.

Shore was the prototypical Bruin, and his dark obsessions are also a staple of the story. It was Shore who raised to the level of gospel the notion that hockey is a sometimes savage game that can only be played well by stoics who can also sometimes be ruthless. It is a harsh axiom that the Bruins and their fans have accepted. And so there has evolved over the generations a phenomenon that the Toronto sports columnist Dick Beddoes once described as "Boston's virulent hockey psychosis." It begins with Shore, but credit (or blame, if you prefer) must also go to Art Ross, Shore's coach and the team's patriarch. He preached the same message. So did Milt Schmidt, Lynn Patrick, Harry Sinden, and Don Cherry. So does Pat Burns today.

"Style" has never been their priority, and no successful Bruins team has ever been known as "fancy." The Bruins have always seen that distinction as yet

General Manager Art Ross poses amiably with Herbie Cain (4), who set an NHL scoring record in 1944, and Bobby Bauer (17), everyone's pal. But the thorny Ross was rarely warm with his lads. As a kid, Ross was a titan of Canadian sport, commanding $1,000 a game in 1908.

another price that's too great to pay for mere victories. Leo Monahan, who has written about them for a half century, notes, "When teams come to Boston they've always known it was going to be physical, and that was so even when the Bruins weren't that good. Opponents always knew they might win the game but lose the physical battle, and they knew that whatever the result, the two teams would probably end up having to beat the crap out of each other."

This merry band of stevedores formed the Bruins' 1934–35 defense (L–R): Babe Siebert, Gordon Savage, Eddie Shore, Jean Pusie. As a star of the Maroons, Siebert, an ox along the blue line, loathed Shore. But they coexisted three seasons anchoring the defense, while Marty Barry and another ex-Maroon, classy Nels Stewart, led the offense. The constant shuffling of "Trader" Ross kept them respectable through the Depression.

Andy Moog (35) thwarts the Islanders as Glen Wesley (26) covers. An earnest Bruin, Wes is remembered for one shot, which

he missed. Another giddy '90s moment, left, finds Ray Bourque, Adam Oates, and Moog celebrating a playoff victory. In five

Bruins seasons, Oates (12) averaged 100 points and he was one of the Bruins most cleaver playmakers this side of Bill Cowley.

But in the end like Moog, Oats left town on a sour note.

Following Spread: A game of centimeters! Jim Carey's in goal; Ray Bourque's on duty. (1997)

He was nicknamed "Taz" after a cartoon character, the Tasmanian Devil. But it was not amusing to get run over by Terry O'Reilly, as ex-teammate Andre Savard's pained look attests. Andy (rear right) went to the Sabres for Peter McNab, who became one of O'Reilly's best buddies. Another pal, Mike Milbury, said of Taz, "He bleeds Bruins!" while Don Cherry called him "utterly fearless!" In hockey brawls, no player was more ferocious than Taz. But he would never discuss his fights later. A door closed when he left the ice. Taz was complex.

A Canadian writer, Peter Gzowski, who has a rather more sociological slant, has further observed: "No team has held more consistently to a single style over the years than the Bruins. They are as delicate as stevedores. At a poker table, they would be the burly, boisterous redhead in the corner ready to give the first man who says he's mis-played a hand a good rap in the mouth. They seem to take as much pleasure out of knocking someone down as in scor-ing a goal. The Bruins have played the game with a joy through brawling that is as Boston Irish as the 'Last Hurrah.'"

It's a neat analysis that may help explain Green and McKenzie, Terry O'Reilly, Fernie Flaman, and maybe even Stan Jonathan. But it's equally a fact that nonbrawling Bruins, like Dit Clapper, Phil Esposito, John Bucyk, Jean Ratelle, and Ray Bourque, were also the glory of their times. All, and many more like them, commanded respect because they were rugged, honest players who could take the heat without backing off from the trench warfare hockey the Bruins, for better or worse, have always felt compelled to play. "Even my nice, sweet players were plenty tough," Don Cherry likes to say.

Cherry, known as "Grapes," raised the thesis of the Bruins' style to the level of canon law in his stormy five-year tenure as coach. When Grapes took over the Bruins in 1974, Orr was on borrowed time and Esposito, the rollicking scoring machine who copiloted the Big Bads in their rampaging days, wasn't far behind. Grapes and Harry Sinden recrafted the team into a grittier, less star-dominated, relentlessly working-class brigade of warriors who wore their hearts on their sleeves and became known as "the Lunch Pail Gang." Ever reaching for more theatrical extremes, Grapes pronounced himself a latter-day Lord Horatio Nelson and made "Blue," his

beloved English bullterrier, the clan's sym-bol. It seemed grand farce, but it masked a clever strategy that combined bombast and guts to push those Bruins to wonder-ful heights.

No team in any game ever played harder than Don Cherry's Bruins. Now a Canadian TV star never at a loss for words, Grapes remains amazed at that team's work ethic. "I wondered about it a long time and I always found it hard to describe," he says. "But this much I know. You could take a

The postwar Bruins contended, but the war eroded too much essence, and the long slide into mediocrity began. Dumart (14), Brimsek (1), and Crawford (6), along with Schmidt and Murray Henderson, thrash with Toronto stalwarts Syl Apps (C) and "Wild Bill" Ezinicki.

journeyman like Dennis O'Brien, who played and failed for four teams, and make him a Bruin and suddenly he is a different guy. I saw it happen again and again. I think it must have had something to do with the sweater." Grapes's Trafalgar was a fabulous game in Montreal where, had it not been for the 30 seconds when he had too many men on the ice, the Lunch Pail Gang would have won the Cup in 1979. Only the Bruins could have lost a Stanley Cup because they had too many men on the ice.

> ## "If you don't believe that Bruins Hockey is roughhouse, rock 'em–sock 'em hockey, then you haven't watched them . . ."
>
> **—Charles Pierce**

Some have wondered if their devotion to a Viking ethos, with its quaint attachment to Old World virtues, has set the Bruins up for more falls than triumphs. A decade ago, the writer Charles Pierce appealed to the Bruins to change their style on the grounds that the Lunch Pail era as well as the Age of Shore are long gone. "The Bruins seem determined always to prove that they don't back down, a point ultimately that is neither relevant nor in great dispute," Pierce lamented, adding: "If you don't believe that Bruins Hockey is roughhouse, rock 'em–sock 'em hockey, then you haven't watched them over the past 47 years during which they have won two Stanley Cups." Pierce wrote those words as the Bruins were being swamped by the utterly new-age Edmonton Oilers in the 1988 Cup Finals. Since then the Bruins have tried, at least halfheartedly, to change, and now it has been 57 years during which they have won two Cups while experiencing, as well, an identity crisis. The notion holds that the Bruins must always be "bruins" even at the risk of remaining prisoners of their past and hostages to their historical image. It is quixotic.

According to the legend, when grocery mogul Charles Francis Adams obtained the franchise for 15 grand in a deal brokered at the Windsor Hotel in Montreal on October 12, 1924, he first sought out a coach, who turned out to be the imperious Scotsman, Art Ross, and then set about the task of naming his team. He settled, with the help of his secretary, on "Bruins," after deciding that was the critter that most conformed to his criteria. It was "an untamed animal whose name was synonymous with size, strength, agility, ferocity, and cunning."

They said it couldn't be done. But when he decided to seize the bit, no-nonsense owner Jeremy Jacobs needed only two and a half years to bring the FleetCenter (right and following spread) to fruition in a $160-million deal, privately financed in its entirety. Of course, some curmudgeons still grieve over "the Gahden."

Indisputably, and for three-quarters of a century, the qualities of size, strength, agility, and ferocity have consistently characterized the team Adams founded. But the fifth attribute, "cunning," is another matter. It's a quality that's too subtle for them. The Bruins have always believed that the shortest distance between two points is a straight line. Even when it means having to go through the boards, head first.

1992 N. H. L. 75th-Anniversary Jersey

1977 Jersey

1956 Coaches' Sweater and Jacket

Brown and yellow were their original colors because they were the colors of founder Adams' Brookside stores. The first jersey featured a not-so-menacing three-legged bear, which didn't make Shore and Hitchman any less foreboding. Coaches Patrick and Schmidt favored the spiffy coat-sweater in the '50s. Bruins myth holds that the jersey has a mystical quality that can make a man tougher.

1949 25th-Anniversary Jersey

1939 Jersey

1929 Jersey

1995 Hockey Gloves

1920s Skates

Dit Clapper's 200th-Goal Stick, 1941

Byron Dafoe's Goalie Mask, 1998

The vintage skates help you appreciate early swifties like Mickey "the wee Scott" MacKay and Nels Stewart. That's Gerry Cheevers' "ghoulie" mask (left). Whenever he took a shot off the puss, trainers Dan Canney and Frosty Forristall etched new "scar tissue" on the thing. The stick delivered Dit Clapper's 200th goal in 1941.

Dit Clapper's 1939
NHL All-Star Jersey

BOURQUE 77 77

Ray Bourque's 1998
Canadian Olympic Jersey

In these times, old sports heroes never die. They simply become "collectibles." The trading cards list for about a grand on today's bull market. Also displayed are Milt Schmidt's '47 all-star garb, Ray Bourque's '98 Olympic jersey and Dit Clapper's jersey for a 1939 all-star game staged for Babe Siebert's family after the ex-Boston and Montreal star drowned.

Milt Schmidt's 1947 All-Star Jersey

THE BIRTH OF THE GARDEN

In their formative years, 1924–28, the Bruins played at the Boston Arena. It was compact and grim, but Symphony Hall was right around the corner, so the neighborhood had a certain élan. Who benefited most from this cultural alliance—the boys in Serge Koussevitzky's world-famous band or the scrappy icemen of the young and raffish NHL—is unclear. But they seem to have coexisted rather well. The prestige of the arrangement not withstanding, owner Charles Francis Adams, an astute maestro of the bottom line, became restless. The rent irked him and he wanted his own ice palace. And then along came Tex Rickard, the fabled boxing promoter, who had just conjured from his boundless imagination New York's Madison Square Garden. A bombastic fellow, Rickard dreamed of building six such grand emporiums, his "string of pearls." Adams and Rickard agreed on a five-year lease for $500,000, a lot of money in the Roaring Twenties.

Ground was broken on Boston and Maine Railroad property off Causeway Street, between the city's West and North Ends, December 3, 1927. An astounding 50 weeks later the Boston Garden was up, looming as large and as imposing as some pyramid along the Nile in the minds and hearts of the fans of that relatively simple time. A fight card, featuring local favorite "Honeyboy" Finnegan, formally opened the building, November 17, 1928. Three nights later, the Bruins christened it with the help of an estimated 17,000 gleeful patrons who stormed the place, charging the gates and smashing barricades in what may have been the wildest opening night in cultural history. Clif Keane was there.

Then a mischievous 16 year old from Dorchester, Clif grew up to become the Boston GLOBE's irascible "Poison Pen," one of the most acerbic and entertaining reporters in the annals of Boston journalism. Clif recalls:

"I hooked school that day and got in line for the 50-cent seats in the second balcony about noon. They lined us up in the alley along the side of the building, and when they opened the gates at five o'clock it looked like the Oklahoma land rush. Guys were kicking and clawing and climbing over each other trying to reach the first row of the second balcony, which were choice seats for a half a buck. You would have thought there was a fire. It was 10 stories to the top; 10 flights of stairs, 13 steps to a flight, a total of 130 steps. I counted them one time. And you ran all the way up, taking four steps at a time all the way to the top of the building. But it was always worth it. Especially that first night."

The Canadiens were the Bruins' honored guests when the Garden opened in 1928, above, and when it closed in 1995, right. But in between, they were rarely such charming company. They met in 18 playoffs between the middle of World War II and the end of the Cold War. And 18 times, the Canadiens won.

Merely surviving the evening was no small achievement. It was chaotic. A newspaper the next day read: "Security guards, caught unaware, were trampled as the giant wave of humanity fought their way to the Garden. Women were overcome and fainted, and it was not until an emergency call was made for extra Boston police, that the frenzied mobs dispersed. Paid ticket holders got caught in the rush and were tossed aside in the mad scramble." As for the game, the Bruins lost to Montreal, 1–0, as the Canadiens quickly asserted their particular genius for ruining an otherwise lovely evening at the "Gahden." Clif Keane continues: "Sylvio Mantha got the only goal on a flip from the right face-off circle that snuck past

Cecil "Tiny" Thompson. It was 70 years ago and I can still see that puck going into the net. I was so mad, I walked six miles all the way back to Dorchester even though it only cost a dime on the trolley. Sylvio Mantha! I cursed him all the way home."

But the evening had one more prophetic feature in terms of establishing the mood of the building and its long, loud love affair with the Bruins. An apparent late goal by Dit Clapper was waved off by officials, precipitating an angry display by fans who showered the ice with debris, briefly renewing fears of a riot. The most vehement protest came not from the lower boxes where men and women in evening clothes and dress wraps lounged, but

from the working class sections; notably, the second balcony. The hegemony of "the Gallery Gods" was being declared. Equally rowdy and profane, loyal and knowing, the Gods seized the second balcony that night and held it to the very hour the Garden closed 67 years later. In the Bruins following, which has been rich, varied, and colorful, the Gods have served as both grand marshals and court jesters. The sorrow of the so-modern FleetCenter, which became the Bruins' home in 1995, is that there is no longer a place for the Gods.

Interestingly, there's no record of precisely when they became known as "the Gallery Gods." But it seems to have been no later than the early '30s.

"Tuesday night was hockey night in Boston," Clif Keane says. "Half the house looked like it had come to a wedding instead of a hockey game. People dressed to the teeth, and there were no overalls allowed; thank you very much. Nobody spat at the players or even swore at them. It was pretty high class." But as was the case with so many of Boston's institutions then, sharp class distinctions existed at the Garden. There was an upstairs and there was a downstairs. And they were very different worlds.

The really lofty fashion statements were made in the rinkside seats where people could be seen and admired, which was entirely the point. The late Tom Fitzgerald of the GLOBE,

Rocket Richard exploded at the Garden March 13, 1955. The Bruins' Hal Laycoe, above, mainly famed as the NHL's only bespectacled player, grazed Richard with his stick, and when Richard discovered he was bleeding he went berserk. "Hal really bugged Rocket," Johnny Peirson recalls. "There was something festering between them back to the days they played together." That "something" was politics. Laycoe was English, while Richard was a fierce Quebecer. In the brawl, Rocket belted linesman Cliff Thompson. Weary of Rocket's tantrums, Clarence Campbell suspended him for the rest of the season, provoking a riot in Montreal that resulted in carnage on St. Catherines Street and 70 arrests. Left: Facing the Canadiens in 1960, the Bruins had Gendron, Burns, Hillman, and Pronovost. The Habs had Geoffrion, Beliveau, Harvey, and Plante. It often wasn't close.

a student of manners and mores, once observed: "It was a much more stylish crowd back then. People still dressed for dinner in those days, and it was not unusual to see women in long gowns and men in black ties coming from restaurants. You'd see the toffs in chesterfields and derby hats. There was still quite an Ivy League influence then. Of course, it was different upstairs." Usually seated in the middle of all the downstairs splendor in Box One was owner C. F. Adams dressed in a camel's hair polo coat and a gray felt hat, the very portrait of the man of affairs for his times.

People of influence remain intense Bruins followers to this day. But the gliteratti faded away after World War II. Downstairs got democratized and infiltrated by people from all classes, or even no class. In the last 30 years of its service, snobbery was the least of the Garden's burdens. But upstairs, nothing changed. It became a darker and more dingy place as the Garden aged, but the Gallery Gods, who at their height numbered about 1,500 partisans, only got more and more protective of their turf. For 30 years, seats

were sold on game day, with the line for big games forming at 1 P.M. and the stampede for the first-row seats ever a spectacle. "But I never saw a fight up there," says Clif. "Not once."

It was worth the effort. In the front row you literally hung from the roof, separated from eternity by a thin rail. Hovering directly over the ice, you could see the steam coming off the players as they labored below, and the sound was enveloping. The price of this arresting experience, exalted by a company of characters Charles Dickens could not have dreamed up, rose from only a half a buck during the Depression to about three bucks at the height of the Bobby Orr era. After the war, the Gods formed their own union. Under the stewardship of the devout Roger Naples, they awarded a much-coveted trophy every season to their favorite player. They developed a fierce comradeship. They attended one another's weddings, christenings, retirements, and wakes. They ministered to one another when there was sickness, passed the hat when someone was broke, banded together in many causes. But always at the core of their existence

was a passion for hockey and the Bruins.

The Gods did not so much watch the game as sit in judgment of it. They would pass on the worthiness of players like the aficionados of bullfighting. Thumbs up, you were okay. Thumbs down, you were meat. And their verdicts were final. In the '50s, the Gods decided high-scoring Don McKenney was too stylish, so they nicknamed him "Mary" and eventually hooted him out of town. McKenney was redeemed in Toronto, where he earned a Stanley Cup ring with Punch Imlach's Leafs, who were hardly a namby-pamby outfit. But if the Gods had misjudged McKenney, they never apologized. To them, elegant players, no matter how gifted, were suspect. They favored hitters like Fernie Flaman, disturbers like John McKenzie, brawlers like John Wensink, and the young Teddy Green. Only a few truly gentlemanly players who disdained rough stuff won their hearts. Hall of Famers Jean Ratelle and John Bucyk were among the best examples, both being near technically perfect players and so fundamentally sound they were in another orbit. The Gods, who above all knew their game

cold, recognized excellence. On the other hand, there was the case of Bill Quackenbush, a fine early '50s defenseman who also graces the Hall of Fame. He made the mistake of once playing an entire season without picking up a single penalty. Such discipline was a tad beyond the comprehension of the Gods. "He was a Lady Byng guy," says Leo Monahan. "And the fans wanted Lady Bang."

They were merciless. In the early '60s, when the Bruins were the punching bag of the league, Orland Kurtenbach was one of the foremost defenders of the colors. A big fellow, Kurtenbach could bob and weave and

jab on skates like Willie Pep and was obviously the Gallery Gods' kind of guy. But then one season when he was struggling more than usual Kurt made the mistake of complaining to Leo Monahan that his slump was somehow linked with the astronomical tides. "It's too early for me," said Kurtenbach, "I just can't get going until after Christmas." His lament ended up in the headlines of Leo's tabloid. When Kurtenbach skated onto the ice the next game, the Gods—some of them wearing Santa Claus stocking hats—greeted him with the singing of "Jingle Bells," the mocking tone rising with each chorus. Not long thereafter, Big Orland and his pugilistic skills were sent packing to Toronto. The Gods had struck again.

The Night the Garden closed: a bittersweet auld lang syne

Sunday evening, May 14, 1995, the Boston Garden got shunted aside like an old war horse because that's what she had become. Many people who did not bother to show up to say good-bye that night thought it was about time and a good thing. But most of those who were there weren't so sure.

Boston basketball fans, who mainly come from other places, never liked the Garden. Rock concert devotees, whose opinions were immaterial, always hated it. But hockey fans, who had the strongest local ties, understood that the mood of the gothic old barn perfectly matched the mood of their game. The creature comforts of the fancy new arena were not their highest priority. So the last game at the old building was for them bittersweet.

Making it the more so was the fact that their boys were not going out in style. By the spring of '95, the Bruins were a fading team at the end of an era. But few were willing to recognize the fact, let alone admit it. After New Jersey's upstart Devils got done with

them in the opening round of the 1995 Stanley Cup Playoffs, the confusion about the point would be considerably lessened. It had to happen, maybe. But the timing was awful. The Devils came into the Garden with a 3-1 lead in the series. All three wins had been shutouts. They had been dominant. The Bruins had been docile. Still, few believed the Bruins would roll over like whipped dogs on this of all nights. They were facing elimination in what would be, if they lost, their last official game in their fabled den where they had historically been—if hardly always the best—surely the most feared team in the game, generation after generation. It was reasoned their sense of history would oblige one last bellicose display.

I walked the place for old time's sake between the periods. The swells were not on hand. There were no dandies in tuxedos and sleek ladies in

Three Bruins defenders—Quackenbush, Armstrong, and the bespectacled Laycoe—cope with the Leafs' Teeder Kennedy line in '52.

long gowns lounging rinkside, as there had been when the place opened over 66 years before. Three of the sky boxes, where corporate high rollers usually watched while swigging scotch, were empty and dark. The last reprise did not draw the smart set.

But the diehards were there. The Bruins' core constituency of sturdy working-class characters, dressed in their Bourque and Neely and Oates jerseys, were all over the place. They were terrific—weeping and singing and taking pictures of one another in their jerseys. I bumped into a chap about 40 who was wearing a ridiculous chunk of foam rubber shaped like a puck on his head. Not knowing what else to say, I murmured, "Enjoy the evening." He smiled and replied, "Ciao!" He was a bloomin' sophisticate in a puck head. "Perfect," I thought. In another corner there was a man in a wheelchair, and sleeping next to him was his huge golden retriever wearing a dog's body sweater emblazoned with Cam Neely's number 8. Would I see them in the new building, I wondered? Sure! From the second balcony,

looking down through the usual haze of blue smoke, the old place looked almost rather pretty.

So the end neared and the Bruins were only down 3–2, and you braced for that last cosmic roar from the depths of their tradition that would spare them the indignity of closing the building on such a whimpish note. But it didn't come because Neely was but a shell of his former self and Bourque was tired and Oates wasn't equal to the moment and the rest of them lacked the wherewithal. Sixty-six and a half years of consistently raucous hockey ended sheepishly as the Bruins staggered off, heads down, while the Devils, who didn't even exist the last time the Cup was raised in the old building, were waltzing around like they invented the game. You didn't know whether to feel sorry for these Bruins for having come

to this state or be mad at them for having offered so little protest. It was hard to take.

Diehards, of course didn't want to leave. I found Tracy and Guy Husbands lingering with their friends in the standing room behind Section 92 at the east end. They had been coming for years to the same spot, game after game. They had courted there. All their Section 92 friends had come to their wedding. It was a familiar story. And they didn't want to leave.

But there would be no allowances for sentiment this night. With enough cops on hand to clean up the Bronx, the premises were cleared in what seemed record time, and there was an empty feeling walking away, with the din receding and

the blue lights of the police cars flashing in the night. It was not the way it should end, you felt. It had been too flat, too mournful.

Four months later, September 26, 1995, all of that was rectified. They had a party. They called it "the Last Hurrah." All the old gang showed up, and a half-million people would have come if there had only been a place to put them. It was mellow in the special way that only hockey people, among sportsfolks, can be mellow. And when Normand Leveille, who was so tragically struck down as a teenager, came out for a bow, there wasn't a dry eye in the house. This was the coda, the Garden's final show. And it was splendid.

THE PLAYOFFS AND CHAMPIONSHIPS

CHAPTER TWO

The Bruins have five Stanley Cups to their credit, won by essentially three different teams in three different eras. However, in a fittingly New England twist laden with a Calvinist sense of punishment, sorrow, and loss, the Cups that should have been won but were squandered have been even more riveting tales. Nothing has come easy because, it has generally seemed, that's what the Bruins with their keen sense of regional irony insist upon. It's been their good fortune to have a core constituency for whom winning is not everything. Like their team, Bruins fans have believed the game is a passion play, and that the play's the thing, in the end.

Charles Francis Adams must have sensed all that when in a flight of fancy he went after a franchise for Boston after falling in love with the pro game at the 1924 Stanley Cup Finals between Montreal and Calgary. While not of the penultimate Adams clan, C. F. did have a magical New England name and a lot of Yankee pluck going for him. He was a practical man with keen business acumen, axiomatic

Don Sweeney, an otherwise amiable Harvard man, runs an opponent. You don't have to be from the set of "Slap Shot" to fulfill the role. Rick Smith is a college professor. Pat Egan was a smiling Irishman. Al Pederson never said "boo." But if you play defense for the Bruins, you have to "hit"! It's quite simple.

for one whose fortune was based on a grocery chain. But he was also one of that distinct breed, then very much in flower, known as "sportsmen." They abounded then, colorful characters named Ruppert and Yawkey, Wrigley and Veeck, Pyle and Rickard, and even Vanderbilt. They loved to wheel and deal and be seen at all the games, and C. F. Adams was decidedly one of them.

After founding the Bruins, Adams would become an owner of the local racetrack, Suffolk Downs, and the local National League baseball team, the ever woebegotten Braves. C. F. was a real "player" and he reveled in it, but that did not mean he was a fool. Like any good grocer, he had a reverence for the bottom line. Which is why his Braves experience, in partnership with the lovably Dickensian Judge Emil Fuchs, almost drove him daft. As a Braves owner in 1935, he helped bring Babe Ruth back to town, however briefly and unwisely. But such amusing moments in baseball were few and far between. The Bruins were different. First, the price was right. Fifteen grand, the NHL admission fee, was cheap even in 1924. More important, he had total control and therefore the option of doing things his way,

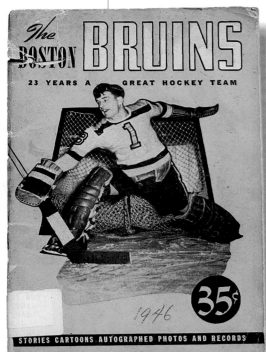

which is why the Bruins became his most profitable and satisfying sporting property. His first hockey decision was his best. He landed Art Ross, forever to be known in the Boston press as "the dour Scot," as his general manager. Ross was no charmer but he was hockey royalty as a player, referee, and former coach at prestigious McGill University. Above all, he was brilliant and as much a devotee of the bottom line as Adams, therefore an ideal partner. The league they were joining was another matter. In 1924, the National Hockey League was a shaky and provincial combine of four eastern Canadian teams. The Bruins would be the first American professional team: a bold step. But Adams, a shrewd judge of markets, recognized vast potential.

As it had been evolving since the 1860s, hockey was an amalgam that drew elements as well as inspirations from a number of tribal games, including lacrosse, hurling, soccer, shinny, and rugby—all of which were rooted in the rich ethnic diversity of New England. The game had followers in both the region's ruling establishment and its working class. By 1916, Harvard was a collegiate power. When the Crimson met Princeton, led by the fabled Hobey Baker, it was a huge event. But hockey was flourishing even more in the wild and woolly amateur-industrial circles, which were called "shoe box leagues" because imported ringers were secretly paid with cash promoters carried about in shoe boxes. Adams and Ross not only proposed to tap into such enthusiasms but to raise them aboveboard. It took the well-connected Ross only six weeks to compose a team, which included such luminaries as Carson Cooper, Jimmy Herberts, and Farmer Cook. "Professional hockey could well become higher class entertainment," spouted a Boston newspaper.

LONGEST GAME

Two of the longest games in sporting history have resulted in painful Bruins losses in playoffs 57 years apart. They played six overtimes for naught against Toronto in 1933, but more excruciating was their triple-overtime loss to Edmonton in game one of the 1990 Finals. The Oilers of Messier, Tikkanen, and company were capping their dynasty. But Mike Milbury's Bruins had Ray Bourque in his prime, Cam Neely at his healthiest, a hot goalie in Andy Moog, and the inspiration of having eliminated Montreal. For a shot at the Cup, they needed to ambush Edmonton in the Garden opener. Bourque scored twice but the Oilers tied it late, and it remained deadlocked past midnight and through two extra periods. Whereupon it got freaky.

It was mid May. The old Garden was a sauna. Fog banks hovered over the ice, interrupting play. The combatants were gasping. Bruins marksman Craig Janney, an arty but fragile B.C. boy, had to be shipped to a hospital and placed on IVs. Then, three minutes into the third overtime, the lights dimmed, plunging the building into an eerie twilight. But it would not be a reprise of the infamous "Lights Out" game in the 1988 Finals against Edmonton; merely a circuit breaker kicking in to relieve the system and prevent a meltdown. For 25 minutes we sat there in the semidarkness while the lights cooled and the clock rolled past 1 A.M. It was another Garden Classic destined to end predictably.

Garry Galley dogs an Edmonton foe in the course of the long night's journey into defeat.

They had one great chance to win it. In a frantic siege around 1:15 A.M. Glen Wesley had the puck unimpeded with an open net yawning 30 feet away. He could have tapped it past Bill Ranford, who was down and out. The weary crowd was already soaring. But Wesley, a gifted if too thoughtful chap, blasted the puck instead and it was high, seemingly landing in Chelsea. He had the whole ocean to aim for and he missed. "Wes never really got over that," the Bruins' Man for All Seasons, Nate Greenberg, laments. "It haunted him." It also still haunts Nate, among others. Moments later, the Oilers' Petr Klima, a talented but lazy Czech who hadn't played all night, raced to the Bruins' net on a three-on-two break and whipped the puck past Moog, ending their dreams of an upset. It was 1:22 A.M. and the Bruins have not been as close to the Cup since.

In the 1933 debacle, the Bruins were the power while the Leafs were the underdog, although with their Conacher-Primeau-Jackson "Kid line" and the lethal defense pairing of Clancy and Horner, they were no pushover. In a five-game series, four went to overtime and the finale was a scoreless gem until two in the morning. Even more amazing, the eventual goat was Eddie Shore.

It was grueling. After five overtimes, the coaches, Art Ross and Conn Smythe, bitter foes who never agreed about anything, proposed to settle the issue by a coin flip because their players were half dead. But NHL President Frank Calder nixed it. Instead, he said, they should play without goaltenders. So they bore on, with goalies. At 4:46 of the sixth overtime, in the 165th minute of play, Shore had the puck at his blue line. He'd been on his skates six hours and was addled. He dithered, slighty losing control, and the Leafs' Andy Blair pounced on the puck. Blair spotted tiny Ken Doraty streaking to the net. His pass to Doraty was perfect. Tiny Thompson, who had made 111 saves in the finest goaltending of his stellar career, never had a chance.

Shore was humiliated. He had enemies, many in Toronto. They didn't let him forget it.

For all of their greatness, Shore (left) and Hitchman (right) were no more popular than the swarthy, lantern-jawed youth they are flanking in this 1930 pose. George Owen was born in Ontario. But his dad became an M.I.T. professor, and George went to Harvard and also starred in football. When he became one of the Bruins, he made them socially acceptable to the "carriage trade." George gave them six fine years on defense, then graduated to big business, in the Harvard way.

They opened December 1, 1924, at the nearly sold out Boston Arena by beating the Montreal Maroons, 2–1. Smokey Harris scored their first goal. A number of scraps, provoked by the Maroons' thumper, Punch Broadbent, enlivened the proceedings. Whereupon they promptly lost their next 12 games and finished the season in last place. One year later, the Western Hockey League folded and dispersed its players. By luck of the draw, the Bruins were able to purchase a 24-year-old defenseman from Edmonton for $25,000. He was an unsmiling, compact, balding fellow named Eddie Shore.

THE FIRST STANLEY CUP 1929: HOCKEY COMES OF AGE

Art Ross was not an easy man nor, by all accounts, a very pleasant one.

But he knew his stuff. By the third year of their existence, the Bruins were in the Cup finals. Eddie Shore, an instant star, was only the foremost of the ultimate Hall of Famers Ross swiftly brought to town. Rugged Sprague Cleghorn, a very British sporting hero quite worthy of his name, was their first captain. He gave them instant respect

Rare among early Bruins stars, little Harry Oliver, right, was stylish and mild-mannered even when he played in the lawless Western League. With Perk Galbraith and Marty Barry he formed "the Thunderbolt line." His crafty playmaking groomed Barry as a prolific scorer.

and led them to a bruising showdown in the 1927 Cup Finals. They lost to Ottawa, but not before leaving their calling card in the deciding game in a vicious stick-swinging joust that had to be quelled by Canadian bobbies. The stalwart Lionel Hitchman, long Shore's quiet defense partner, also arrived in 1926, as did Harry Oliver and Perk Galbraith. Dit Clapper, who would become beloved, came aboard with Norman "Dutch" Gainor and Frank Frederickson in 1927. Cooney Weiland and the estimable goalie Cecil "Tiny" Thompson followed the next season along with Harvard's George Owen and Dartmouth's Myles Lane, thus delivering that touch of "higher class" that had been promised. And 1928 also brought the wondrous new Boston Garden to which the Bruins, by dint of their style, immediately warmed. The puzzle was complete.

More to the point, the team's persona had been firmly established. A 1926 game with the Maroons led the GLOBE to comment: "In its wildest moments, the Great War was a tea party compared with the wild hockey battle that exploded tonight." That term "war," very vivid less than a decade

Art Ross had a talent for creating great teams of the Roaring Twenties, like the '29 champs, who had an affinity for hot roadsters. Captain Hitchman stands guard at the rear while Eddie Shore in his fashion dominates the front row. In their 1929 championship year, the Bruins intriguingly mixed old gunfighters Cy Denneny, Frank Frederickson, Perk Galbraith, and Mickey MacKay; young stars Shore, Hitchman, Clapper, Oliver, Thompson, and Weiland; college boys George Owen of Harvard and Myles Lane of Dartmouth. Certainly an accomplished group of men. But nobody, not even Shore was bigger than Art Ross. He was a scholar who devised the first helmet, standardized the puck, and designed the goal net used to this day.

after the butchery in France, was frequently invoked. On another occasion, it was written: "The game itself was a hell-raiser. Sticks were carried high and there were illegal checks, charging from behind, deliberate socking, and countless trips and cross-checks that furnished plenty of color and excitement." The roots of the tradition had been struck. Ross had cast the team's image forever in the likeness of the grim and implacable Eddie Shore. It was rock-ribbed defense, anchored by the fierce Shore-Hitchman pairing and the dauntless little Thompson in goal, that carried them all the way in the 1928–29 season. They allowed only 52 goals in 44 games, led the league in wins, and won their division by 17 points.

Somehow in the playoffs, they managed to tighten the defense yet another notch. In the opening round, they met a Montreal Canadiens team that featured certified legends Aurel Joliat and Howie Morenz plus a goalie, George

> ## "It was like the American army returning from overseas after the Great War."
> —THE GLOBE

Hainsworth, who had posted 22 shutouts in 44 games. The Bruins rolled through them in three straight. Weiland scored the winner in each of the first two, both 1–0 shutouts by Thompson. Game three in Montreal was an angry affair. Lurid press reports claim Hitchman—the Bruins' captain—played much of the game "with blood streaming all over his face from a tremendous gash on his head." They won 3–2. Shore had the winning goal. Ross, a Montreal native whose contempt for French-speaking Canada was legend, was exultant, or at least as much as the "dour Scot" ever allowed himself to be.

Even then, beating the Canadiens had signal import. All along the route of the long, festive train ride back to Boston, people gathered on the platforms of tiny stations in Vermont and western Massachusetts to wave and shout hosannas. Said the GLOBE, "It was like the American army returning from overseas after the Great War." When they arrived at Boston's North Station, they were, according to press accounts, "engulfed by a merry mob . . . that tossed them around good-naturedly after pushing its way through a large detail of police."

In the wake of all that, the finals were a bit of an anticlimax, although the New York Rangers had superb characters like the Cook brothers, Bill and Bun; Frank Boucher; and the menacing Ching Johnson, whose Attila the Hun–like bearing made him their answer to Shore. Game one was another Thompson shutout, 2–0, with Clapper and Gainor scoring the goals. For the thrilling second and last game, police expecting mayhem were massed like infantry: three hundred on foot, another couple of dozen on horses, plus one hundred railroad cops. The game was tied, 1–1, with less than two minutes to go when Dr. Bill Carson, the part-time dentist, took a pass from Harry Oliver, swept by the mighty Johnson, and flipped the puck past John Roach, bringing the Cup to Boston. It was called "the $25,000 goal" because that's what it meant in terms of bonuses in the pockets of the lads.

FRED HITCHMAN

Art Ross hobknobs with his supberb "second line" of (L–R) Mel Hill, Bill Cowley, and Roy Conacher. It was 1939. Cowley's line

outscored the more celebrated "Kraut line" that championship season. As a coach, Ross was a brilliant motivator. Milt Schmidt

recalls: "He never ranted behind the bench, but between periods he'd stand at the end of the dressing room smoking an Old

Gold just staring at us. And slowly he'd zero in on his target with what we called 'the bad eye.' Then he'd tap his head where

the brain sits and say, 'USE IT!' That's all he'd say and all he had to say."

Mainstays of the '30s (above) included gritty little Cooney Weiland (left), a key character on three

Cup teams, and the redoubtable goalie Cecil "Tiny" Thompson (right), who over a decade had a

goals-against average of 2.05. Weiland later became an institution as the Harvard hockey coach for

20 years. Right: That's Dit Clapper (left) daring to ride Eddie Shore (2) about his thinning hair. Shore

looks amused, does he not? Nonetheless, Flash Hollett (12) and Jack Portland (8) think it's funny.

"TINY" THOMPSON

Five days later, the champions were celebrated with a magnificent banquet at the Copley Plaza's Swiss Room. It was as tony as it got in 1929 Boston. Himself, James Michael Curley, the bombastic and already legendary mayor, was the featured speaker. Each player received $500 in freshly minted gold cartwheels, which if prudently stuck under a mattress would be worth at least a half million dollars today. The players presented C. F. Adams with a two-foot-high bronze bear, imported from Russia. The wine flowed long and late. During these days in the spring of 1929, as the Bruins were winning their first Cup, Ferdinand Foch, marshal of the Allied Expeditionary Forces in the Great War, lay dying in Paris. Charles Lindbergh was becoming engaged to Anne Morrow. Admiral Richard Byrd was in the throes of his most spectacular adventure, trekking across the frozen wastes of Antarctica. In the battle for space on the front pages of the newspapers, the Bruins had elbowed their way into the ranks of such movers and shakers. In five years, hockey in New England had made it.

William "Flash" Hollett (12) was a gift from noted Toronto philanthropist Conn Smythe, who didn't recognize that Hollett's offensive skills were rare. In eight Bruins seasons plus two with the Wings, Flash set NHL scoring records for a defenseman that lasted until the Age of Orr.

The next year, the Bruins were billed as near unbeatable. They roared through the regular season winning 38 of 44 games, 15 more than second-place Montreal. Weiland broke the scoring record and had 43 goals. Clapper had 41. Thompson won his first Vezina Trophy, awarded to the best goalie. Shore set a record for penalties. And in the playoffs, the mighty Bruins were promptly ousted in two straight by the Canadiens, led by Morenz and a certain Albert "Battleship" Leduc, who had scored, in the regular season, only six times. It was a refrain that would echo down through the years.

CUPS II AND III, 1939 AND 1941: THE AGE OF THE KRAUTS ON THE EVE OF WAR

Entering the 1938–39 season, the Bruins were an intriguing blend of remarkable relics and raging youth. Amazingly, Shore, Thompson, Clapper, and Weiland, the core of the 1929 champs, were still with them. But if each, to varying degrees, had endured brilliantly, there had been no more Cups, a fact that had begun to prey upon Ross, the gloomy Scot, who was still very much in charge.

Shore was still Shore. The indisputable fact was verified the previous season when he rebounded from a fractured vertebrae that would have finished most players to win his fourth MVP Hart Trophy. Others mellowed with age, but not the relentlessly countercultural Shore. He was meaner than ever. Charming by comparison, the gallant little goalie Thompson had verified his worth the previous season by winning his fourth Vezina Trophy. Tiny was beloved by everyone but the Bruins' tightfisted management, and therein lies the rub. The season started with Shore still a bitter holdout. He was always tough to sign and a backbiter of management, which made his behavior in later years, when he became the most ruthless skinflint owner in the entire hockey cosmos, if not the history of sport, all the more ironic. It took the interventions of NHL czar Frank Calder to get Eddie to accept a $7,000 contract. He was, of course, worth at least seven times that amount, even with the Depression still in flower.

Money was also at the root of Thompson's lingering discontent. He had never quite forgiven management for brutalizing him in a 1932 contract dispute. In the money wars back in those good old days, the owners knew how to play hardball and they did not suffer suspected malcontents gladly. They would take it—most reluctantly—from Shore, but not from anyone else, not even the much-adored Thompson. On November 29, 1938, a week after Shore capitulated, Ross—with the gleeful assent of Weston Adams, who had replaced his dad as owner—sold Tiny Thompson to the Detroit Red Wings. There was no spinning by the always candid Ross. The money obtained plus the money saved on Tiny's contract, he said, would be used to buy more players. It was balderdash. They already had a wagon. It would be years before there would be any more significant purchases. There was outrage in the streets, as well as on the team. The illustrious Clapper threatened to quit. It was said to be the foulest transaction any Boston team had pulled since infamous Red Sox owner Harry Frazee sold Babe Ruth to the Yankees. That's how highly Tiny Thompson was regarded in Boston.

But if the deal was spiteful and mean-spirited on the part of ownership and callously handled by Ross, who had the sensitivity of a blacksmith in such matters, it was also brilliant. Ross knew that for a fraction of the cost he could replace Thompson with a better goalie who was ten years younger. His name was Frankie Brimsek. He was in the nets the next game, took a loss, and got roasted by the fans. But over the next month he won a dozen games, six of them shutouts. Suddenly, he was being called "Mr. Zero"! The laconic Brimsek had one more huge advantage going for him. He was that rarest of NHL players at the time, an American, hailing from a remote and frigid up-country Minnesota town named Eveleth. When Frazee sold Ruth he replaced him with bums. When Ross and Adams sold Thompson they replaced him with Mr. Zero. By the spring, Thompson was forgotten while the shy Slav had 10 shutouts, breaking the NHL scoreless streak record, formerly held, ironically, by Thompson, and becoming the first player to win both the Vezina and the Calder (Rookie of the Year) trophies as the Bruins were rolling to their second Stanley Cup.

Somebody must have slipped brandy in taciturn Frank Brimsek's tea to induce this affable pose. He was not your basic party animal or publicity hound. A quintessential goalie, he was shy, remote, high-strung, finicky about his equipment, and superstitious about most everything. He never forgot the roasting he got when he replaced Tiny Thompson in '38, even though he swiftly turned the jeers to cheers with an astonishing six shutouts in seven games.

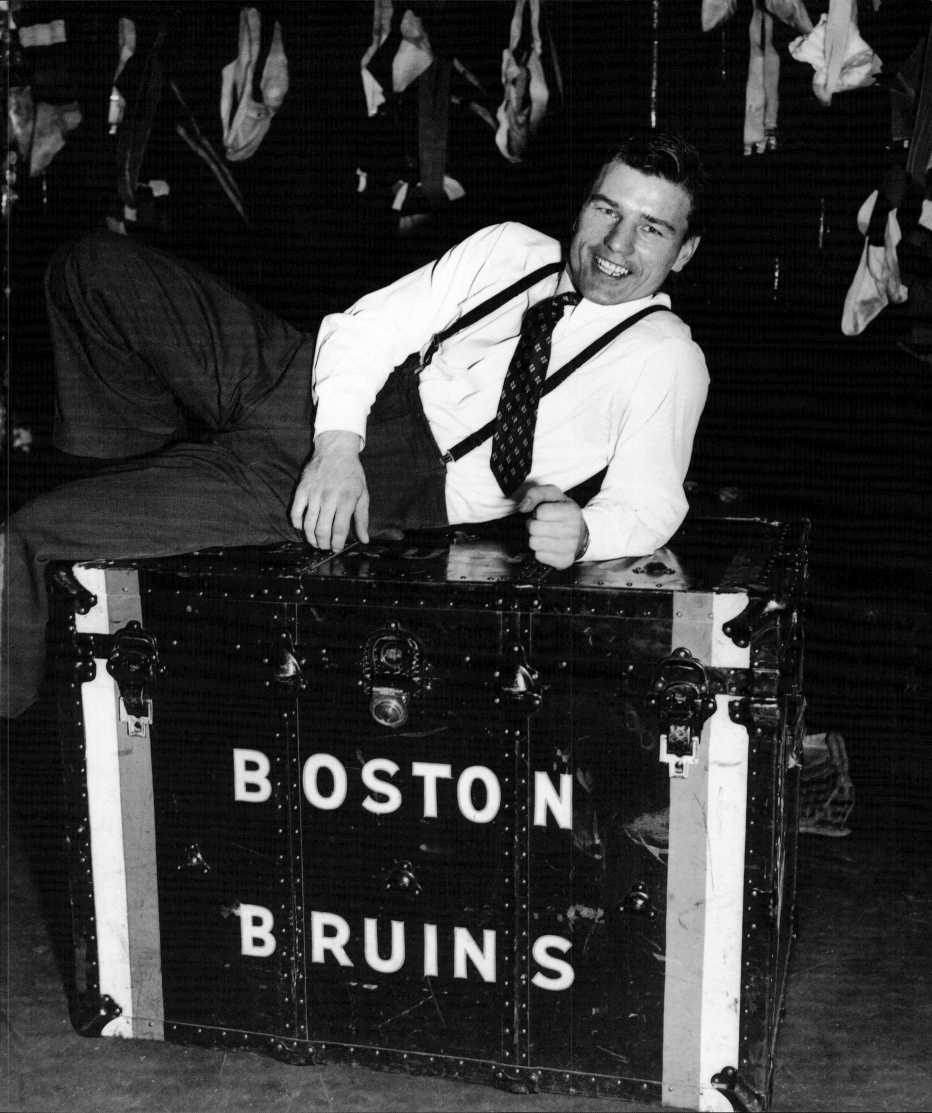

Too Many Men on the Ice

The seventh game of the 1979 Stanley Cup Semifinals between the Bruins and Canadiens, famed as the "too many men on the ice" nightmare, was a riveting passion play portraying sport at its most dramatic. In splitting six games, the team with home ice always won, so the Canadiens, with their mystical Forum seething more than usual, had the edge. Yet Boston dominated most of the way. Wayne Cashman, who'd risen to an impressive sobriety and maturity after becoming captain, scored twice and Rick Middleton added another; all three were set up by matchless Jean Ratelle. They led 3–1 with nine minutes to go.

Penalties had been a volatile issue throughout the series. Don Cherry was endlessly denouncing the alleged pro-Montreal bias with operatic arias from the bench, while Harry Sinden had been spotted stalking the Forum's bowels with the suspected intent of kicking down the door to the officials' room. It was the usual uproarious burlesque, but on the call that turned the game around they had good reason to bellow. Responding to a swipe by Bob Gainey, Ratelle, arguably the cleanest

player in hockey history, pushed back and was penalized by ref Ron Meyers. It was a moronic call, unthinkable under the circumstances. Naturally, the Habs pounced, with the breathtaking Guy LaFleur setting up Mark Napier and Guy Lapointe within a span of two minutes to tie it. But these Bruins were gallant. Ratelle made an exquisite move, outwitting Larry Robinson and slipping the puck to "Nifty" Middleton, who darted around the cage and slid a backhander past a befuddled Ken Dryden, and it was 4–3 Bruins with 3:59 to go.

Here is where the gods had their little joke. With two minutes left, Boston got called for having one more skater on the ice than the rules allow. They were unquestionably guilty. The extra skater—Donnie Marcotte—was out there for what seemed a half hour. Linesman John D'Amico looked sad when he signaled the infraction, and even Meyers acted reluctant to make the call but he had no choice. You can't field ten men in baseball or a dozen in football, and you can't skate six

men plus a goalie in hockey. It's that simple. Nor was it Marcotte's fault. As the game's best defensive forward, his orders were to shadow LaFleur, to be on the ice whenever "the little Flower" alighted. In desperation, Habs coach Scotty Bowman was triple-shifting his ace, creating constant confusion for Marcotte. The "fault" lay entirely with Cherry, who

admitted it. "Hey, I grabbed two other guys and pulled them back. Otherwise, we would have had nine men on the ice," Cherry later quipped, fighting back the tears with sarcasm. "Maybe I should have let them go and we could have really done a number."

Gentleman Jean Ratelle got huge respect. One day, the lads were being rowdy in the locker room. Cheevers barked, "Watch your language; Ratty's here!" He wasn't kidding.

Having received a monumental break, the Canadiens still had to capitalize. It was like the Red Sox–Mets 1986 World Series classic, when Bill Buckner's blunder brought about Boston's ruin. But had it not been for a gallant Mets uprising, Billy Buck never would have had the chance to screw up. You have to give the adversary credit sometimes, which was the case in Montreal. Graced with a power play, the Habs still had to score, and LaFleur, who was on another planet all night, insisted upon it. He took the puck deep in his own end, and with the Bruins falling back too cautiously, he curled up ice. Building speed through the center zone he fed Jacques Lemaire, who tapped the puck right back to the Flower, who had so much thrust on the ensuing slap shot that I'm not sure anyone actually saw the puck go by Bruins goalie Gilles Gilbert. In net because Gerry Cheevers was under par, Gilbert played the game of his life that night. But no mortal could have stopped LaFleur's blast.

Wisely, Leigh Montville and I went down to ice level and watched the ensuing overtime with our noses pressed against the glass to Gilbert's left. The OT was stupendous. Dryden made unconscious stops, two of them, bang-bang and point-blank off Marcotte. Gilbert, thrashing on the flat of his back, stopped LaFleur and Steve Shutt on shots he could not possibly have seen. But these were the Canadiens they were up against. The outcome was inevitable. Middleton had a semi-breakaway, but the elegant Serge Savard got back, broke him up, curled, and made a perfect pass into the center zone, which Mario Tremblay received in full gait. Tremblay had a half stride on Bruins defenseman Al Sims, and that's all he needed because on the other side of the ice, Yvon Lambert had a half stride on Brad Park. If the glass hadn't been there, Monty and I could have reached out and grabbed Tremblay as he threaded the puck across to the crashing Lambert, who pushed it past Gilbert even as Park, arriving a split second late, flung himself at Lambert and landed on his face. Some things you never forget, and every detail of that moment is forever etched, as is the memory of the noise in the Forum that night. It was colossal.

It was the most heartbreaking loss I ever saw a pro team sustain, nor did I ever see a team weep more in its locker room—and it may have been the toughest team I ever covered. Cheevers hadn't played. But it was still left to him to express the agony of it. "I look around this room and I want to cry," he said. "I never saw a team try so hard and not win. I want to cry for them. I never saw a team give so much of themselves." He could go no further, being too choked with tears. Montreal proceeded to the Cup, cakewalking over a mediocre Ranger team, as the Bruins surely would have done had they won. Within a week Cherry was gone, his wacky dispute with Sinden proving terminal. An era was over and the Bruins, as of this writing, have not come as near to the Cup since.

"Nifty" Middleton scored 402 goals for Boston and became superb on defense, which no one who saw him as a Rangers rookie will ever believe.

Brimsek was the final piece in the composing of a great team, but the key had been put in place three years earlier with the forming of the Kraut line. There is the danger of rhapsodizing excessively about Milt Schmidt, Woody Dumart, and Bobby Bauer because even 60 years later they still seem too good to be true. They were three noble teenage innocents when they ambled from Kitchener, Ontario, in the mid-'30s, three strapping lads bonded by their German heritage and their love of hockey. It was their decency along with their tough, honest, and ethical play that made them immediate favorites. They stayed on the scene for decades and the wonder of it is, they never really changed.

In 1930, the "Dynamite line" of dashing Dit Clapper (left), tiny Cooney Weiland (center), and the urbane Dutch Gainor (right) scored 102 goals. Right: A decade later, Jack Crawford irked traditionalists by wearing a helmet all the time. But he could hit with the best of them, so he was forgiven.

With the Krauts and Brimsek and Clapper, Shore, and the now-fading Weiland, the irascible Ross had woven a deeply balanced team. Bill Cowley, who old-timers tell you was the best playmaker of all time, came aboard in 1935. Mel Hill, who with good reason would become forever known as "Sudden Death," arrived in 1937, to be followed by Roy Conacher, scion of an aristocratic hockey family, in 1938. A couple of blocky, hard-nosed defensemen, Jack Portland and Jack Crawford, and a rushing rover named Flash Hollett completed the package. The Krauts were their heart and soul, but the Cowley-Conacher-Hill line was the league's most dangerous offensive unit. They lost only 10 of 48 regular season games, finishing 16 points ahead of their nemesis in that era, the Rangers. The playoffs were another matter.

Historians have called the Rangers-Bruins Stanley Cup semifinal that ushered in the ominous spring of 1939 the finest series ever played, and if all of that is impossible to measure, it was almost certainly the most dramatic in Bruins history. The teams were ideally matched: the Bruins as usual being the gritty, hard-nosed, mauling club while the Rangers, as usual, were the smooth, swift, stylish type, although hardly pantywaists. No team then could be and survive. The Rangers were coached by Lester Patrick, the Connie Mack of hockey, and they featured stirring brother acts—Colvilles (Mac and Neil) and the Patricks (Lynn and Muzz) plus Bryan Hextall, Alfie Pike, rugged Babe Pratt, scrappy Phil Watson, and a little goalie known for his valor, Davey Kerr.

In 13 days, they played the equivalent of nine games—four of them stretching lengthily into overtime—while rolling on the train together back and forth six times between the two Gardens built by Tex Rickard. If the games were superb, the train trips must have been something else. Game one went to the last seconds of the third overtime before Cowley fed Hill to end it at 1:10 in the morning. Ross called it, advising Cowley to look for the lightly regarded Hill who had scored only 10 goals all year, because the Rangers were hounding the much more prolific Conacher. Adding to the sweetness of it, Hill was an ex-Ranger who, when he was dropped by Patrick, was told: "You'll never make it kid. Go home and find something else to do." One all-night train ride and a

Unruly fans stalked the moment. One fired a bottle onto the ice. Another winged a potato at a Ranger. Both were arrested.

day later, they played game two in Boston, and again it went into overtime before Hill ended it again on another pass from Cowley. They won game three routinely, 4–1, and headed back to New York looking for a sweep.

But the Rangers gallantly rose to the moment. The key, according to New York authorities, came when Muzz Patrick beat up Shore "fair and square," whereas Boston-based experts insist Shore was mugged by at least four Blueshirts. Nevertheless it's clear the Bruins got rattled. The usually stoic Brimsek raced to Shore's defense waving his stick like a war club and had to be restrained by Clapper. They lost 2–1. In game five, back in Boston, angry fans showered the ice with garbage, tossed tin cans from the galleries, and fired firecrackers into the air. It was a rousing evening that again stretched into overtime before the Rangers' Clint Smith scored. Back in New York, they got blown out, departing to an operatic chorus of "Choke . . . choke . . . choke" as sung by the only fans in the league nuttier than the Bruins' own.

It set the stage for an epic game seven in Boston. In the second period, Ray Getliffe scored for the Bruins. Three minutes later, Muzz Patrick tied it, and it remained tied in the raw aura of true sudden death for the next three and a half hours. Clapper brawled with Ranger roughneck Art Coulter. Unruly fans stalked the moment. One fired a bottle onto the ice. Another winged a potato at a Ranger. Both fans were arrested. Finally, midway through the third overtime at 12:35 in the morning, Shore mounted a rush, feeding Conacher, who was rebuffed by Bert Gardiner. But Cowley pounced on the puck in the corner and dumped it in front, where an enterprising Bruin was waiting to stuff it home. That Bruin was, once again, Mel "Sudden Death" Hill. It was a helluva nickname to have to drag through life but Hill sure earned it.

In the finals, they met a Toronto team that had persecuted them throughout the '30s but was now aging and totally dependent on freckle-faced Turk Broda, yet another of the era's fabulous goalies. There were subplots. Ross had long feuded theatrically with Toronto's equally irascible boss, Connie Smythe, while Shore and Leafs bully Red Horner had been the bitterest of foes. But nothing came of any of it as the Bruins romped in five uneventful games. Shore was no longer the mainstay, but he was still the greatest of the

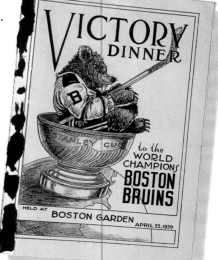

Mel "Sudden Death" Hill (left) and smiling Bill Cowley proclaim their intention of sweeping Toronto in the 1939 Cup Finals.

Hill scored heavily with the Leafs during the war, but he never topped his Bruins overtime heroics. The clean and classy

Cowley was the definitive playmaking center. His deft touch at setting up his wings led BOSTON RECORD columnist, Bud

Gillooly, to famously declare: "Cowley made more wings than Boeing." When he retired in 1947, he held the NHL record for

assists, 353, and most points, 548.

The 1939 Stanley Cup champs, one of the fire wagons of NHL history. Front row (L–R): Roy Conacher, Mel Hill, Charlie Sands, Cooney Weiland, Milt Schmidt, Gord Pettinger, Flash Hollett. Back Row: Frank Brimsek, Jack Crawford, Eddie Shore, Woody Dumart, Bobby Bauer, Dit Clapper, Bill Cowley, Jack Portland, Ray Getliffe. Cowley had the most points, 42. Conacher the most goals, 26. Brimsek won the Vezina and the Calder Trophies. And Eddie Shore, in his last full season with the Bruins, went out on top.

scene stealers. The record book says there were 16,891 people at the final game at the Garden. But one authority—the late Russell "Ace" Booth—claimed there were at least 20,000 there, the wildest of them literally hanging from the rafters. "The scenes following the sounding of the final bell almost beggar description," the GLOBE reported. "Connie Smythe hopped the dasher and ran over to congratulate Art Ross while the players shook hands. Firecrackers rent the air. Fans screamed and shouted and the band broke into 'Paree.'" It was when it came time for League President Calder to present the Cup that the crowd realized Shore was not there. Bedlam followed.

Never easily given to joy, Shore was still nursing his salary grievances. He was also—quietly—already plotting to extricate himself from the Bruins and stick it to Ross and Adams. It was in this fine spirit of petulance that he raced to the dressing room when the game ended and refused to return to the ice for the ceremonial presentation of the Stanley Cup. But the crowd would have none of it. They stomped, whistled, and chanted "We want Shore" over and over. The chant swept the building. At center ice the players massed around captain Cooney Weiland, understanding fully there was no way they could accept the Cup without Shore. Milt Schmidt, who was in the eye of the storm, recalls: "The crowd simply would not let Mr. Calder present the trophy until Shore came back on the ice." Team officials begged him to come out. Ushers and stickboys begged him. Cops begged him. But he wouldn't budge. Finally, according to an account that may or may not be fanciful, some newspaper pals reached him with the impeccable logic that if he didn't relent, there would probably be a riot. "The uproar was stunning when Shore finally came out," says Schmidt. "The crowd gave him such an ovation it made goose bumps run up and down your back and I can still feel them." So, in a scene that might have been borrowed from Wagner, they at last got to skate the Cup around the building. Nine months later, Shore was gone—traded to the New York Americans, who would soon go out of business, for Eddie Wiseman and a bundle of cash.

With or without Shore, it was a terrific team. They won the 1939–40 regular season title with Schmidt, Dumart, Bauer, and Cowley as four of the league's top five scorers. Weiland had taken over as bench coach, allowing Ross to focus on the salary-crunching G.M. duties he so loved. Under Weiland, offense was supreme. They became much more wide-open in style, and they paid for it dearly in the playoffs. In a much-ballyhooed rematch with the Rangers, they took a 2–1 lead then lost the last three games as little Davey Kerr shut them out three times. It was profoundly shocking as well as—it should again be noted—a familiar theme in Bruins history. Doubtless sensing that gathering war clouds made a "win it now" policy imperative, Ross beefed them up with the acquisition of Terry Reardon,

This was as cool as it got in 1940. The reigning champs are rakish in their pricey lids and fancy jackets, which one of the lads tells me the frugal Adams ownership allowed them to pay for themselves. Front (L–R): Jack Crawford, sporting a new wig, and the Krauts, Milt Schmidt, Bobby Bauer, and Woody Dumart. Back row: Flash Hollett, Art Jackson, Frank Brimsek, Roy Conacher, Jack Shewchuk, and Dit Clapper.

After finishing first in the 1939–40 season, they were upset by the Rangers in the playoffs. But the next year the Bruins redeemed themselves, running roughshod over the pack. In one stretch they went 23 games without a loss.

The 1938–39 champs endured major upheavals. Eddie Shore had a bitter contract squabble, then Tiny Thompson was auctioned off, making way for Frank Brimsek. That's Mr. Zero making a save on his back in one of his first Garden games, while Bill Cowley (10) and his mates observe. You'll note Shore (2) is wearing a helmet. After the Ace Bailey incident in 1933, he often did (see page 121). Some whispered he was getting "soft" but none dared say it to his face.

Following spread: Contemporary fans express their joy. Only the dress code has changed. In the '30s, Blue line Club members wore derbies and spats to the games.

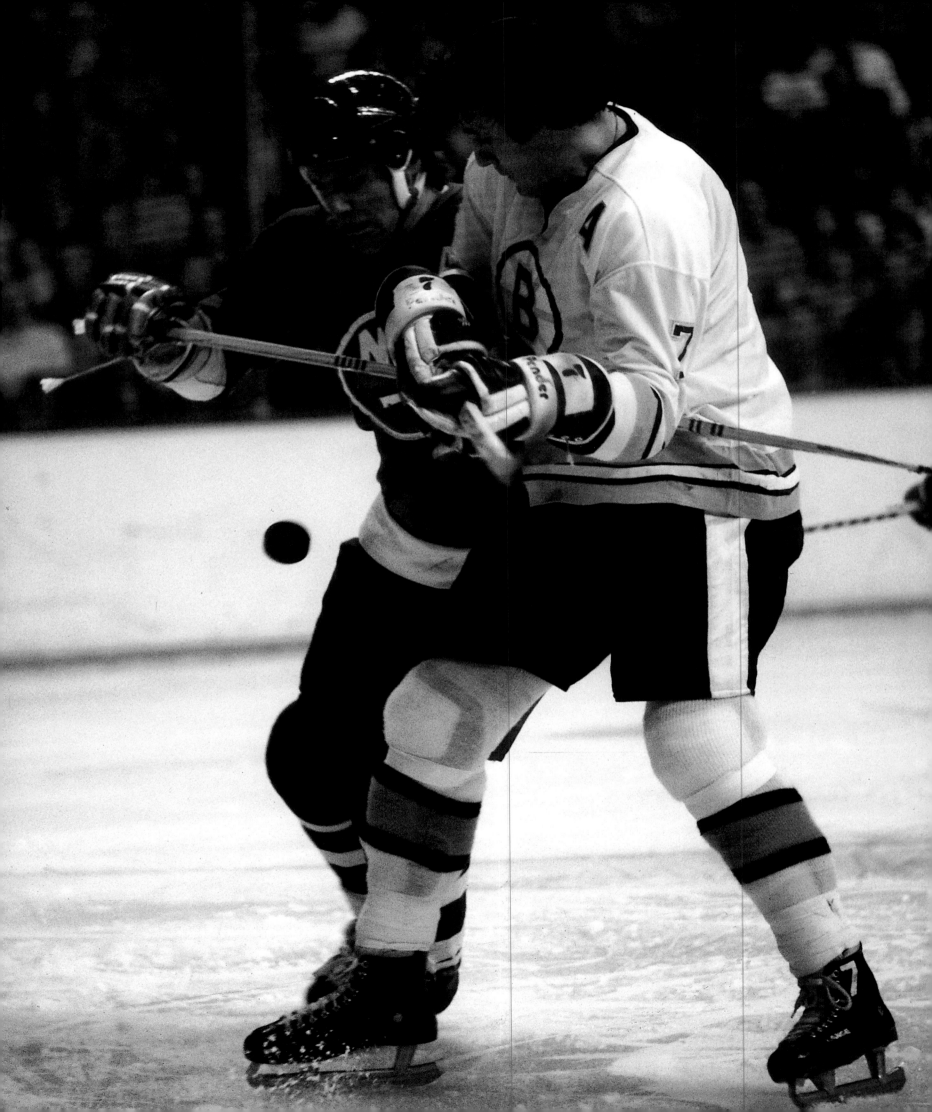

Herbie Cain, Des Smith, and Art Jackson, kid brother of the Leafs' fabled Busher Jackson. The result in the 1940–41 season was another first-place finish, another raft of scoring records, a record for assists, plus a scoring title and a Hart Trophy for Cowley, the Lady Byng Trophy for Bauer, and another Stanley Cup.

Once again, all the drama came in the first round, where the Bruins had to come from a game down to beat the superb Broda and the Leafs. Led by Hollett, Wiseman, and Schmidt, they waltzed past the outclassed Red Wings in the finals. On the long train ride home from Detroit with the Cup, they could exult in being at their peak and still just kids while knowing as well that the party was over. For Pearl Harbor was but eight months off. It was an unusually fine team. "We got along so well," Schmidt now says. "And that meant an awful lot. We didn't have cliques on that club, and if there was any sign of one, you had fellows like Dit Clapper who would put you in your place in a hurry. And you listened to those people. It was a 'Yes, Sir–No, Sir' deal in those days. You didn't use any foul language, and it wasn't 'Art Ross,' it was 'Mr. Ross,' and it was 'Yes, Dit' and 'No Dit.' They were gentlemen. You never talked back to them. They said something and that was it." It was a different age.

CUPS IV AND V, 1970 AND 1972: THE BIG BAD BRUINS

On the other hand and at the very opposite extreme of the social and cultural scale, there was the colorful and curious team that became lionized as "the Big Bad Bruins." It's an era defined by the arrival of Bobby Orr in 1966 and the departure of Bobby Orr in 1976; these events demarcated the period like two giant bookends. Immortal as he was, however, Orr needed help, and he had plenty. After a long, agonizing rebuilding, a superb team was in place when in June of 1967, Milt Schmidt engineered an astounding trade with Chicago that brought forwards Phil Esposito, Ken Hodge, and Freddie Stanfield to Boston for the stunningly meager price of Gilles Marotte, an overrated defenseman;

Pit Martin, a nice center who was too small; and Jack Norris, a goalie who promptly disappeared. It was the greatest trade in the team's history; possibly, in terms of its consequences, the most one-sided in the history of the game.

If as a team, the Big Bads were roughly together for a decade, their run of excellence and dominance was much shorter and nowhere near as long as it should have been. By the 1968–69 season, they were ready to challenge for the Cup. After the 1971–72 season, their best days were behind them. The story of the Big Bad Bruins still fascinates brooding New England because it is as much a tale of paradise lost as paradise gained.

Still, what should most be remembered is the simple fact that this team was enormous fun. Every day was a holiday. It was the Gashouse Gang on skates. They were Rabelaisian. They didn't beat teams, they engulfed them. Everything they did reeked of excess. They were rowdy, vulgar, and vain. But to their adoring legions, they could do no wrong. In a region that considered itself sophisticated, macho hockey, worthy of the movie SLAP SHOT, became downright stylish. There was never a team that was more the toast of their town than the Big Bad Bruins. "They were wild all right," says Leo Monahan, who reported on their shenanigans on and off the ice from start to finish. "And they weren't always in training all the time, if you know what I mean. But they all stuck up for each other. If one was in a fight, they all were in a fight. And even their gentlemen were tough." By their definition they never scored enough goals, won enough fights, ruffled enough establishment feathers, or had enough laughs. Maybe in some odd psychic way they sensed the clock was running and it wasn't going to be a long season. They were perfect for their times. Irreverence was then very fashionable.

At the height of their celebrated hex over Boston, Montreal stopped them from winning four straight Cups. In 1969, a couple of key face-offs that were lost and a fabulous finish by Jean Beliveau were the thin margin of difference. In 1971, they astounded all of sport with a regular season romp through the league that faintly resembled the German army's prance through Belgium the last couple of times they went to war. Brave men found it hard to watch whenever the schedule matched them with one of the newly formed expansion teams. For most of the game's history, scoring 100 points in a season had been hockey's equivalent of the four-minute mile. In 1971, the league had four 100-point men and all of them—Esposito (152), Orr (139), Bucyk (116), and Hodge (105)—were Bruins. And yet the Canadiens, whose top scorer, Jean Beliveau, had

Only hockey players vie for a symbol, the Stanley Cup, and have their names emblazoned on such a bauble for all time. That it is thereby a Holy Grail to them is evident in the radiance of (L–R) Milt Schmidt, Tom Johnson, Bobby Orr, and Harry Sinden. It was Mother's Day, 1970.

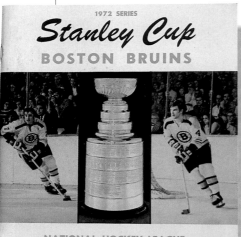

exactly half as many points (76) as Esposito, knocked them off in the opening round thanks mainly to the acrobatic works of a quite intellectual rookie goalie out of Cornell, Ken Dryden. If you're looking for more irony, consider this rarely noted fact: The Bruins had owned the rights to Dryden when he was only 16, before he went Ivy League and became so smart as well as good. But wily Sam Pollock, boss of the Canadiens, had suckered the Bruins into a trade in 1964. The Bruins got the rights to Guy Allen and Paul Reid, both of whom would never be heard of again, and the Canadiens got Dryden. No one in Boston seems to remember who made the deal or why, but it happened.

What might have been, though, is secondary to what "the Big Bad Bruins" did do, which was to win the Cup in 1970 and 1972 with as much bombast as any team has ever won it. In 1970, they struggled in the opening round against the Rangers. They were nasty games between two teams who loathed each other, and when the series was tied at two games apiece, some vicious critiques in the New York newspapers charged that the Bruins, for all their bluster, lacked guts. It was the spark they needed. They won the next ten straight, finishing off the Rangers and then sweeping both the Blackhawks and Blues, outscoring them 40–17. Their odyssey ended with Orr's lyric glide through

Bruins history crested with the second great civic tribute that drew a hundred thousand revelers to City Hall Plaza, May 13, 1972. Wayne Cashman did a memorable imitation of a drunken Johnny Cash, and this time Mayor White dumped a bucket of beer on Johnny McKenzie.

the air after sweeping the puck past Glenn Hall on Mother's Day.

Two years later, their trek ended in New York. They had pounded two rather weak teams, the Maple Leafs and the Blues, to get to the finals while the Rangers were beating the much tougher Canadiens and Blackhawks. But along the way, New York's superb center Jean Ratelle broke his ankle, leaving all of the burden of Ranger leadership on the sloping shoulders of Brad Park. They were again mean games, and I have the particular memory of Park clawing like an alley cat with the Bruins' Wayne Cashman, who was superb in that series. The Bruins won it in six games, with Orr again winning the Conn Smythe Trophy as MVP.

The plane ride back to Boston that night was chaotic. We landed at 2:15 A.M. with everybody on board standing, clutching a beer. "Hang on," yelled the pilot. And then we were down. When they opened the doors, thousands of people were swarming the tarmac and the gate areas and the long hallways of the terminals while dozens of overwhelmed police stood by and watched. So elated was the mob, members of the media were even borne off on their shoulders. The state police had to rescue Orr, Esposito, and Sanderson, sneaking them off into the night. In the rush to the airport, people had abandoned their cars in tunnels and along the highways. It was absolutely mad.

Two days later, more than one hundred thousand people gathered to pay them tribute at City Hall Plaza, and at the height of the reveling, a reeling Cashman teetered on the mayor's balcony and tossed his socks to the hysterical mob below. The cheers Cashman received for his display of bravura were deafening. It was the zenith of the Big Bad Bruins.

THE BRUIN GREATS

CHAPTER THREE

Remarkably, in 62 of their "first" 75 seasons, the Bruins were either coached or managed by either Art Ross or Harry Sinden. Ross was fully in command from 1924 to 1954; Sinden, from 1966 to the present save for a two-year sabbatical in business.

EDDIE SHORE

Hockey history brims with tales of rugged, square-jawed, laconic characters who come out of cold and distant places to turn the game on its ear. For the Bruins, Eddie Shore was the prototype. In his time, he was known as "the Babe Ruth of Hockey." But he was not a Ruth. There was joy in Ruth's game, as well as excellence and majesty. In Shore, there was plenty of excellence, but no joy. He was more the Ty Cobb of Hockey: peerless on the battlefield but also lonely, haunted by his own myth, and driven by forces near mad. As was the case with Cobb, the game served a need in Shore that had little to do with aesthetics or pleasure. It's revealing that many of the great stories about him have much to do with pain, his ability to inflict it and, even more, his capacity for enduring it. Eddie Shore suffered a lot. It seemed to be the way he measured his courage, which, like an old gunfighter, he was compelled to do again and again. Shore was the Shane of hockey, minus the sensitivity. He hasn't played in six decades and has been dead two, yet the complexities of Eddie Shore are more fascinating than ever.

Shore came out of the bitterly remote farm country of Saskatchewan, thoroughly groomed in the old-fashioned religion of the Protestant ethic. In a splendid SPORT magazine profile in 1959, Al Silverman wrote: "When he was 12, he was put to work allocating stock to various tenant farms. He had to drive a four-horse team, pulling a wagon loaded with 150 bushels of grain 40 miles a day. But he loved the work and he developed a strong, muscular body." The first sport he mastered was bronco busting. He had little interest in hockey as a kid; he didn't play it seriously until he went off to an agricultural college in Manitoba, when his brother Aubrey dared him to give it a try. So he did and promptly became a fanatic. When the fortunes of the family farm dipped, he opted for a professional hockey life, a stunning show of chutzpah for one who had been skating only a couple of years.

He planted the seeds of his legend one night with an amateur team, the Melville Millionaires, when he sustained a broken jaw, a broken nose, and the loss of six teeth yet refused to leave the game until he was hauled unconscious into the dressing room. Word of such marvelous derangement traveled fast. He soon became the rage of the fast, fierce Western Hockey League, cementing his image as "a wee bit addled player" who should not be trifled with. He starred with Regina, Victoria, and Edmonton, where he acquired the nickname "the Edmonton Express." It stuck. One night in Edmonton he played in defiance of doctor's orders with 14 fresh stitches in his thigh, popped them open, kept right on playing, and finished the game with his pants soaked in blood. By 1926, the Western and Pacific Leagues were bankrupting and NHL moguls were circling like sharks. The heaviest spender was the grocery baron from Boston, C. F. Adams. For $50,000 he landed a stable of western stars, sold some to the Rangers and Red Wings, and brought Harry Oliver, Perk Galbraith, and Eddie Shore to Boston. For Adams, who flung nickels around like manhole covers, a rare venture into the money wars had solidified a franchise and acquired a legend for virtual peanuts.

But coach Art Ross exempted no one from the rituals of initiation, so in one of Shore's first Bruins practices he let resident bully Billy Coutu—famed as hockey's dirtiest player and a chap Percy Leary once called "a grisly side of beef"—try to soften up the impudent hotshot from the West. Being cruel came easily to Ross. The legend

Charles Francis Adams (right), lifelong patron of the game, may have paid mightily to bring Eddie Shore to Boston, but he understood the value of a nickel as only a man who began life sweeping grocery stores and ended up owning the First National food chain could. He had money squabbles with Shore and others. His accomplished son, ex-Harvard goalie Weston, Sr., took over in 1936 and was even tougher. Four years later, Shore was gone. Weston's presidency was interrupted by World War II. He was a commander in the navy serving on LSTs. In the '50s, he surrendered control of the Bruins to Walter Brown, of basketball fame. But he came back to supervise the team's rebuilding in the '60s. Weston, Jr., rounded out the clan's ownership in the '70s, until the team was sold to Storer Broadcasting.

Like cavaliers from the age of Louis XIV—battered and bloodied but unbowed—Sugar Jim Henry (left) and Maurice "Rocket"

Richard (center) exchange traditional civilities after Rocket's spectacular goal eliminated the Bruins in the 1952 Playoffs. The

Rocket had been mauled by his nemesis, impish Bruins disturber Leo Labine, the "Haileybury Hurricane," a manic character

who carried his stick at high port. But when you drilled the Rocket you only made him more lethal. In losing 18 straight play-

offs to the Habs in the 45 years from the height of World War II to the end of the Cold War, no one persecuted the Bruins

more than "the Rocket."

claims the confrontations were awful. Again and again Coutu ran the kid—his own teammate, mind you—who, of course, refused to blink let alone budge, until finally Shore was nailed against the boards and left with the side of his face drenched in blood. Coutu had practically severed Shore's ear with his stick. The doctor on duty said it would have to be amputated, but Shore would have none of that. At a hospital, he found a doctor six hours later who was willing to try to sew it back on, and here's where it gets macabre. Shore not only refused anesthesia but asked for a mirror so that he could monitor the repairs and, if necessary, correct them. Even nasty characters like Ross and Coutu could appreciate such stoicism. Years later, the late great Ray Fitzgerald asked Shore what his thoughts

were as the doctor sewed his ear back on his head. "I thought it hurt like hell," Shore replied. "From that moment, the Bruins knew they'd got themselves something special," says Leary. There would be no more "testing" the mettle of Eddie Shore.

So many of the Shore tales are like the ear story, seemingly the kind of folklore that makes Pecos Bill and Paul Bunyon beloved in myth without being taken too seriously. But if anecdotes about Shore have been embroidered, as is always the case with outsized characters, there is little doubt they are essentially true. There's the one about how he got stuck in New York after missing the team train, so he rented a taxi and headed north toward Montreal right into the teeth of a blizzard, and when the driver in sheer terror refused to press on, Shore took the wheel and drove until they landed in a ditch somewhere in Quebec, whereupon Eddie walked to a farm, convinced the farmer to hitch up a wagon and lug him to a train station, arriving 35 minutes before the game, after a 22-hour trek with no sleep— and he went out and scored the game's only goal as the Bruins beat the Canadiens. Wow! And it actually happened. In 1929. Years later Ross described Shore's appearance that night with undiminished awe: "His eyes were bloodshot, his face frostbitten and windburned, his fingers bent and set like claws after gripping the wheel for so long, and he couldn't walk straight. His legs were almost paralyzed from hitting the brake and clutch." And still he played, missing not a single shift. If Shore's grit impressed Ross, it did not keep him from fining him for missing the team train. There was nothing sentimental about the dour Scot.

On another occasion in New York, where bad things invariably happened, Shore collided with a goalpost, broke three ribs, ran a high fever, and ended up in a hospital, from

Not even old age could diminish Shore's ferocity. At the 1974 hockey meetings, Eddie had an argument with Autrey Erikson, ex-NHL defenseman. It ended when Eddie decked Erikson with a right cross. Erikson was 36. Shore, survivor of six heart attacks, was 72.

Proof that Eddie Shore had a soft spot for kids is here provided. But as he aged, his eccentricities only deepened. In his long, colorful ownership of the Springfield Indians he terrorized players, went to lunatic extremes to save nickels—even pennies— and became frighteningly autocratic in his beliefs about everything, on and off the ice. He had strong notions on the effects of sex on athletes. He once assembled the Indians' wives and ordered them to curb relations for the playoffs. Don Cherry recalls, "He yelled at them and he said, 'now you just cut that stuff out!'" Eddie Shore was a character.

which he promptly escaped when he awakened just in time to catch the team train for Montreal, where the next night he scored the winning goal. It was also in New York that Rabbit McVeigh of the Americans tried to hurdle the fallen Shore and slashed him with his skate right across the forehead and bridge of the nose. Witnesses say blood literally gushed from the wound. It was hideous. Shore missed only one shift while they taped him. One night in Montreal, the Maroons, seeking revenge for past Shore abuses, ganged up on him. He sustained a broken nose, a gashed cheekbone, facial cuts, three broken teeth, and two black eyes before being lugged away on a stretcher after getting knocked cold by the evening's last brutal hit. He played the next game. There is no scorecard per se tabulating the wounds Shore piled up in his career, but historian Stan Fischler says: "The best estimates place Shore's total number of stitches in excess of 970. His nose was broken 14 times, his jaw shattered five times, and all his teeth had been knocked out before his career ended.

He barely missed being blinded in both eyes and nearly lost an ear." There were also, of course, the broken ribs and ravaged limbs, and later in life Shore suffered eight heart attacks. But here we are confining ourselves to the cosmetic stuff.

Shore was no conventional goon, and his historical image as a brawler is way off. He led the league in penalties only once, possibly because most sane opponents were more than pleased to give him a wide berth. It is noteworthy that his archfoe, Toronto's Red Horner, was the penalty leader eight straight seasons in Shore's prime. Eddie didn't like to use his fists and was above the circus stuff. But he was a smashing hitter, a master of dirty play, and a "Ph.D." with his stick, which was a finely crafted surgical instrument in his hands. "He was always a little vicious," the Rangers' Muzz Patrick told Al Silverman, "so you had to be sure to get him first. But he never complained when things happened to him."

Frank Patrick of hockey's royal family coached Shore two years, 1934–36, while Art Ross focused on G.M. duties. Shore's skills and devotion made him a joy to coach. But no one bossed him. Milt Schmidt says only two men in the world were not afraid of Ross: Bill Cowley and Eddie Shore.

It was ex-boxer Muzz Patrick, once the official Heavyweight Champion of Canada, who administered one of the worst drubbings Shore ever took. It came in game four of the Bruins-Rangers joust in the 1939 playoffs and almost swung that epic to the Rangers. When Shore, then almost 37, tried to intervene—naturally, with his stick—in some unpleasantness between teammate Jack Portland and the Rangers' pesky Phil Watson, Patrick jumped him and pummeled him. "I could feel his head squash when I hit him" was the way Muzz indelicately described the

> **"The glory of Eddie Shore . . . is that he always triumphed over viciousness . . ."**
>
> **—Al Silverman**

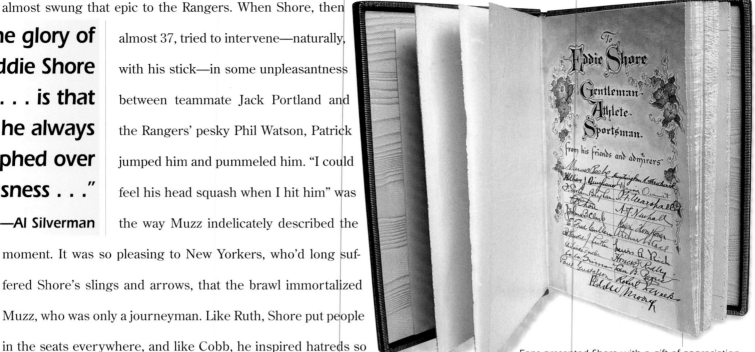

Fans presented Shore with a gift of appreciation

moment. It was so pleasing to New Yorkers, who'd long suffered Shore's slings and arrows, that the brawl immortalized Muzz, who was only a journeyman. Like Ruth, Shore put people in the seats everywhere, and like Cobb, he inspired hatreds so intense they surpassed the games in drama. In a 1934 article for COLLIER'S magazine, Kyle Chricton wrote: "What makes Eddie Shore the greatest drawing card in hockey is the hope—entertained by spectators in all cities but Boston—that he will some night be severely killed." He had life-or-death, decade-long feuds principally with the Rangers' Ching Johnson, the Maroons' Babe Siebert, and Horner of the Leafs. But if opponents loathed him, their respect for him was, in hockey's atavistic ethos, boundless because Shore could take it as well as give it. "He never, ever asked for any quarter" is the way Patrick put it. There's no higher compliment within the tribe.

That does not mean they ever fathomed him or his arrogance, rigidity, and dark view of both life and humanity. Woody Dumart, long his teammate and the most civil, affable, and engaging of sporting gentlemen, recalls: "It was strange, but you'd never see him in any of the cities we visited until game time. Nobody knew where the hell he went. He was a real loner. I used to bunk across from him on the long train trips and I don't remember having a single real conversation with him even after I lucked out and got a lower bunk right next to him." They didn't really know Shore because Shore didn't want them to know him. He was your classic enigma. "The glory of Eddie Shore," Al Silverman wrote 40 years ago, "is that he always triumphed over viciousness—his own and his opponent's." But sometimes, plainly, it was a close call.

The twin pillars of Bruins history who rarely crossed paths meet. Shore liked Orr, but once told Clif Keane: "Orr wouldn't have gotten away with that fancy stuff with me. I would have had the stick ready for him. If he skated around my net, he'd have been in trouble." Amen!

BOBBY ORR

Image is a funny thing. Bobby Orr and Eddie Shore might seem mirror opposites, Shore always being portrayed as a scowling character given to dark moods while Orr, on the surface, seemed inspired, lyric, even ethereal. It's presumptuous for me to make comparisons, given that while I never saw Shore I must have seen two-thirds of Orr's pro games. But in an educated hunch, based on many learned opinions, I'd say Orr and Shore had much more in common than not. The superficial differences of style and appearance aside, both were fiercely possessed and driven men of eerie skills and moods who were also original, revolutionary, and in the end, somewhat haunted by their excellence. Being seen as "unique," as each was in his era, can be as much a burden as a grace. Their most palpable bond, however, was the fact that they were the twin pillars of Bruins history. There is Shore and Orr, and then there is everyone else. That too was a burden.

"Bobby Orr was so good as a hockey player that nobody could describe why he was so good," the estimable Leigh Montville once wrote. It was a dilemma people who talk and write about sports for a living struggled with over and over. Once you agreed he was sui generis, what more could you say? Montville added, "There wasn't any one factor. He simply was 'better,' one grade above everybody else in every area of the game. Simply 'better.'" He could skate better, shoot better, pass better, had more command of everything that was happening, and he looked better doing all of it, and if there was something he didn't do better than anyone else, it was because he hadn't tried, or he figured it wasn't worth the effort. That's what everyone believed, so even if it wasn't true, it might as well have been.

In 1970, Harry Sinden said of him: "This is a helluva statement and I'm sure I'll get a lot of flak about it, but he may be the greatest athlete who ever lived." That was the year Orr smashed scoring records willy-nilly, dismantled the Rangers and Blackhawks in the playoffs, then brought the Stanley Cup to Boston after a lapse of three decades by scoring the clinching goal as he soared through the air against the Blues. Bobby Clarke of the Flyers, one of his most bitter foes, said: "It wasn't fair that he was made to play with us. There should have been a higher league for him to go to." Orr transcended his game much as Babe Ruth did baseball, and Jim Brown did football, and Michael Jordan has in basketball. But Orr lifted the bar of excellence in his game even higher than they did in theirs. As a pure artist—one who came from a different planet and played in a world of his own—he was more comparable to a Ted Williams, Bill Russell, or Gale Sayers. But Williams couldn't play defense, Russell couldn't play offense,

Orr's Cup-winning stick, May 10, 1970

and Sayers's knees were even worse than Orr's. Sinden may have been right. Said Serge Savard of the Canadiens, "There are players, stars, and superstars; and then there is Bobby Orr."

The awe he inspired within his lodge was unreal. One winter night in 1976 we were sitting in a Hartford tavern after a WHA game between the Whalers and the Houston Aeros, who then featured the entire Howe family. Whalers coach Harry Neale, now the beloved Canadian hockey announcer, was there, as was Peter Gammons, who was then laboring for SPORTS ILLUSTRATED, and several battle-scarred Whalers, including the impish Johnny McKenzie, who in his previous existence was known as "the piranha of the Bruins." It was a good group and the conversation was lively, and it eventually turned, as it invariably does when hockey characters gather, to the subject of who was tough and who wasn't. Carefully considered opinions backed with chapter and verse citing famous brawls and extraordinary combat were offered by everyone until finally McKenzie, who knew about the subject if ever a man did, stood up with his beer and announced he was ending the debate. "The best fighter in the history of hockey was Bobby Orr," he declared solemnly. "Nobody had better leverage on his skates and nobody had quicker hands, so he could have licked anybody he wanted to," said McKenzie. "If he wanted to."

> "The best fighter in the history of hockey was Bobby Orr."
>
> —Johnny McKenzie

It was classic "Orriana," the attributing of mythical charisms to him on the assumption that in his omnipotence he must have had them even if he didn't display them. On the other hand, there is the distinct memory of Orr, back around 1969, taking on a notable Montreal pugilist, Ted Harris, who was four inches taller and 20 pounds heavier. Orr pounded Harris as convincingly as Joe Louis pounded Max Schmeling. Nobody at that table that night in Hartford disagreed with Pie McKenzie. As they used to say about Babe Ruth, "All the lies they told about Bobby Orr were true." Teddie Green, his gruff teammate, said of him: "Hockey is a game of mistakes and Bobby Orr doesn't make any."

Proclaiming a new era, the 18-year-old messiah joins the much-touted 33-year-old rookie coach, Harry Sinden, at the 1966 preseason training

camp in Ontario. It was the first week with Orr wearing number 1, not yet having been assigned his mythic number 4, which had last been the

property of a certain Al Langlois. The teenager's averted look was then typical. Painfully shy with adults when he came up, Orr rarely talked

above a mumble and was acutely self-conscious about his skills. But he was never a rube on the ice. In his first game with Detroit, Gordie Howe

sticked him in the ribs. The kid sticked Howe right back. Howe was impressed.

Also in their heyday during "the Age of Orr" were four media stalwarts who have niches in the Hockey Hall of Fame (above L–R): radio's Bob Wilson, the GLOBE's Fran Rosa, and TVs Fred Cusick, who logged an astounding 44 years behind the microphone. The fourth is the estimable D. Leo Monahan, right, whom you'll hear much from elsewhere in this text. Booming Bob lived for hockey and was groomed on the long-gone Olympics as well as the Bruins. Fred telecast the first Bruins national TV game in 1957 for CBS, a 5–3 loss to Andy Bathgate and the Rangers. Fran chased the puck across the GLOBE, covering the epic struggle of Harry Sinden's Team Canada with the Soviets in 1972. But his first love was Orr's "Big Bad Bruins." Of those players, he wrote: "There was no distinction between them. They had an intangible quality that infected the team and made them brothers."

Skilled as he might have been at brawling, that is neither what he did best nor why his genius is recalled so vividly near a quarter of a century after a perverse fate forced him to quit just when he ought to have been reaching his prime. Everybody has his favorite Orr memory. Johnny Peirson, who as Bruins TV colorman during the Orr era often had to explain the inexplicable, thinks his most unreal moment was a rink-length dash against the Atlanta Flames in 1975.

Peirson recalls: "It was end to end plus. Dan Bouchard was in the Atlanta goal. Bobby took the puck behind his own net, came out, pirouetted, and circled behind his net again, and then he rolled down the right side with a burst of speed until he found he couldn't cut in because the defense was pinching him, so he surged around them and then went around the Flames' net so quickly that Bouchard, who was hugging the left post, could not get over to the other side fast enough and Orr just tapped the puck into the open corner." What made it the more amazing was the fact that the Bruins were shorthanded, down a man, and before his rush Orr had held onto the puck for 22 seconds, spinning about in the sort of delicate patterns a 90-pound figure skater would find difficult to perform while the Flames thrashed about helplessly and backed into one another. His coach that night was Don Cherry, and he remembers: "After the goal, maybe the most beautiful ever scored, there was complete silence in the Arena because nobody could believe what they had just seen. It was the only time I ever heard 10 seconds of silence after a goal. Bobby just skated away with his head down because he knew he'd embarrassed Atlanta. At moments like that I used to stand there and get chills." Orr's modesty in such circumstances was always arresting. It was as if he believed it was his responsibility to hold his preternatural skills in check and felt obliged to apologize.

"You didn't need to know a blessed thing about hockey to appreciate Bobby Orr," the late Ray Fitzgerald

of the GLOBE, who had a poetic sense of such things, observed. "You didn't have to be able to distinguish a blue line from a squall line to understand the moves and pivots he made on the ice were tiny works of art. Orr played the game with the grace of a Bolshoi balleteer. He was Nureyev on skates. When he was into his game, the Boston Garden turned into Swan Lake."

My own favorite "Orr moment" comes from an otherwise insignificant game against the North Stars, circa 1971. Again it was an end-to-end beauty, beginning with him winding up behind his own net and screaming up ice like an F-14 shot off a flight deck, only when he reached the Minnesota blue line, he got mugged by their two defensemen. One chopped him high and the other slashed him low. All three went down. Only as he fell, Orr curled, and as the three players rolled in a tangle of legs and sticks toward the corner, Orr reached back, got his stick on the puck, and passed it to a breaking Johnny Bucyk, who simply tapped it past the transfixed North Star goalie, venerable Gump Worsley. There was no way Orr could have seen Bucyk, and yet his pass to him was perfect. He always saw what nobody else could see.

The one thing he couldn't—or wouldn't—do was talk about it. Orr's reticence frustrated the media of his time. He was one of the hottest stories in sports. Public interest in him was insatiable. But getting much more than an "aw shucks" out of him was near impossible even if he knew you, or—rarer still—trusted you. When he came to Boston he was a high school kid who was sensitive about his lack of learning and undeveloped social skills. The shyness was understandable, even charming. But as he grew in sophistication and it became clear he had plenty of native intelligence, his refusal to open up infuriated many media types. But like everything about Orr the issue was more complex than his critics were willing to believe. He was truly shy by nature. The laconic, Jimmy Stewart manner was no act. He had an aversion to boasting and had been raised on the notion that humility graced heroism. He played a game that celebrated modesty in its stars and was rooted not in American but Canadian culture, and there's a difference. He was embarrassed by the fact that he could command more attention than all of his teammates combined. He genuinely wanted to promote them. But he also wanted to protect himself and his carefully crafted

One night as Orr circled his net he got hacked and his stick broke. Orr kept rushing, moving the puck with his skates like a soccer player. As he whistled by the bench, ever-alert trainer Dan Canney tossed him a new stick, and he completed the foray, bringing a hush to the rink. No one had seen that one before.

image that played so well with the public despite its near childish simplicity. Above all, he was determined to keep his private life, which was not lacking in sophistications, very private, and that determination—fortified by a stubbornness that was sometimes almost frightening—became, like many other features of the man, an obsession. Amazingly, he succeeded.

"Nobody was ever beloved in this town more than Bobby Orr," Montville wrote when it came time for Orr to leave. "He was a throwback to the old-time hero that was found only in daguerreotype poses. He loved his mother, drank his milk, helped old ladies across the Expressway. He kept the rest of his life so private that he always was portrayed as Childe Bobby, always as the boy wonder, always in that heroic mold." It was some achievement for an allegedly unlettered innocent. To the last he remained, in the choice phrase of one of the town's testier pundits, "Our Darling Boy!" (the "caps" are his). The most skillful politician could not have managed his or her image better. But he was always more complicated than he wanted us to know.

Not that it really mattered whether he was Tom Sawyer or the Artful Dodger off the ice. The boyish charm, the Byronic aura, the image of the noble and selfless rustic who would lay down his life for his team, would have worn thin soon enough and quickly bored a cynical town in a jaded age had it not been for the works bordering on the divine that he performed on skates night after night even after he had no more cartilage in his left knee and he was bone on bone. He always insisted that to him hockey was pure instinct and that he couldn't explain his magic even if he wished to, but he came close in one of his authorized books when he said: "After a game I would sit in the dressing room and ask myself why I did certain things that night on the ice. Most of the time, I have no answer. I had the puck at one end of the ice and there were two players checking me pretty closely. The next thing I knew, I was alone in front of the goaltender. I honestly do not know what I had done to get there." Which suggests he played in some sort of

dream state. It's often the way it looked. Style was a huge part of it. So was the fact that he played without a helmet and was fully revealed in all of the creative dimensions that made women sigh and men marvel. Sinden, a straight-talking hockey man not given to overstatement, said in 1970, "I think of how I was there on the bench to watch every single game he played his first four years and I realize what a lucky, lucky man I am." Orr rewrote the game's tactics, its theories of offense, its concept of the defenseman, its text on how to play the power play, its conventional wisdom on how to kill a penalty. Said Chris Lydon, the NPR don, "When Orr is on the ice it is his game, not because he dominates it, but because he seems to have invented it."

Nowadays it's fashionable to consider Orr the greatest who ever played the game. In one generation, his legend

He was Hockey's first $100,000 player, then its first career million-dollar player.

has soared, plus he benefits from sentiment. Opinions uttered in 1975 when he was still playing may be more valid. Some examples: The august Herbert Warren Wind, who critiqued hockey for lofty journals like THE NEW YORKER, called Orr "the last of the classic stick-handlers" and "a very inventive player forever devising variations on his variations." Wind saw in Orr's skating something almost metaphysical. To Himself, Eddie Shore, it was his passing that was most impressive. Said Shore, "Orr has the inborn ability to judge how hard to send a pass exactly relative to the speed of the recipient." Red Burnett, a Toronto scholar of particular gravitas, urged caution: "It's stupid to compare different generations," he said. "Today the equipment is better, the ice is better, the vitamins are better. Orr's playing in a diluted league. Instead of eight or ten real good players on a team, you have two or three." And yet, he noted, when you broke down Orr's skills, you found them surpassing. "He can do everything. He has great acceleration, great puck-handling ability, a great shot, the ability to start a play then be in position to finish it off." Burnett concluded he could NOT say Orr was NOT the greatest. The irrepressible King Clancy, hockey's ultimate mahatma, was less equivocal. "Yes, Orr's the greatest with the next best Morenz," King said, referring to the star-crossed Montreal legend Howie Morenz. "But Morenz was a forward and defense is tougher to play. Morenz was faster and more physical than Orr, but not as shifty. I don't see anybody checking Orr and that could be because he's that good a skater." A point that Jacques Plante, the immortal Canadiens goalie, clarified further. "He isn't checked," said Plante, "because too many opponents were burned too often early in his career. They tried to check him and were left deep in their own end." Cutting to the quick, Milt Schmidt offered: "The single most important play is getting the puck out of your own zone. Nobody ever did that as well as Bobby."

Containing Orr by means fair or foul was like trying to lasso a tornado, which Pecos Bill found didn't pay. Orr's speed was formidable, but it was the mercurial moves that made him awesome. When he rushed bowlegged through the zones varying his speed ineffably, defenders backed up before him, frantic in their fear of what he might do next. If they collapsed on him, he would find the open man, or work the give and

Right: **A** hopelessly overmatched foe gets sandwiched by Orr and defensive wizard Donnie Marcotte (21). Orr's offense was so awesome, his defense got overlooked. But he was as good on D as he wished to be and a superb and fearless shot-blocker, to the chagrin of his coaches.

Hugely controversial when he bought the team, Buffalo concessions mogul Jeremy Jacobs, below, then got unfairly mauled for letting Bobby Orr get away. A generation later, he's had "the last laugh."

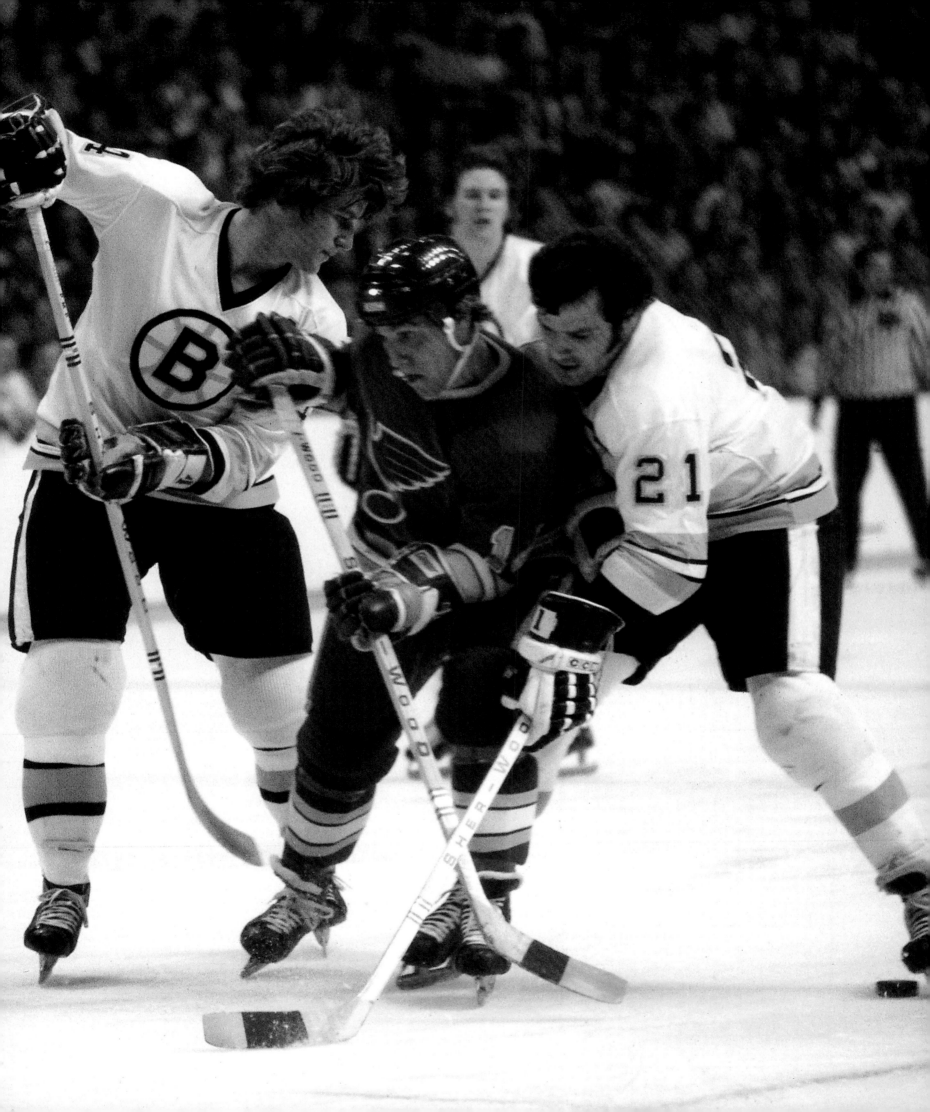

Only Doug Harvey and Eddie Shore challenge Orr as a defenseman. Harvey has the edge defensively, but Orr could skate, stick-handle, shoot, and attack better. As for Shore, Elmer Ferguson, dean of the pundits, told historian Stan Fischler in 1968: "Orr is a better player in practically every way than the great Shore. Eddie exuded drama with his powerful rushes, and he was courageous. But in the mechanics of polished hockey, Orr is greater." And he would get even better! Like Shore, Orr had an eerie threshold for pain. His old roomie, Eddie Johnston, insists he played with separated shoulders and a broken hand.

go, which was his favorite play. If they didn't collapse, he would use them as a screen and bury the shot with his semi-slapper, which, while not that hard, was deadly accurate and released with a quickness that was in itself a sight to behold. While chary of posing as an expert in the company of the hockey divines that have been quoted, my vote for "the greatest" would go to Gordie Howe because he did almost as much for much longer, and I value longevity. But if it's a question of skills, brilliance, originality, aesthetics, artistry, majesty, and theater, my vote would go to Orr.

Nonetheless, this much is beyond dispute: he revolutionized hockey both on and off the ice. With the contracts he signed, guided by an agent who would grossly betray him, Orr broke the feudal grip of the owners, and the players adored him for it. When, at 2:30 in the morning of Labor Day, 1966, the 18-year-old phenom signed a two-year contract with the Bruins for $85,000 aboard Hap Emms's yacht in the middle of Lake Ontario, it was like a fire bell in the night all over the kingdom of hockey. Why, Howe, the reigning divinity who'd been a star 18 years, only made $35,000 that season. "The year after he arrived, I got an eleven thousand dollar raise," McKenzie once chortled. "And it was all because of him." Subsequently, Orr was hockey's first hundred-thousand-dollar player, then its first career million-dollar player. But if he received, he also gave. When he came along, the NHL was rapidly expanding and striving to break from its medieval bonds into the age of television, big bucks, and Madison Avenue mores; Orr gave hockey the hip image it desperately needed, and the owners knew it. When his career crumbled, a grieving league president called it, "the greatest individual loss in NHL history." A cosmopolitan man who picked his words carefully, Clarence Campbell added: "Bobby had more to offer the future of this game than anyone. He generated hundreds of thousands of fans whom I fear will never see his like again." Small wonder that Orr himself looked upon the cruel terminating of his career when he still seemed the indestructible "Childe Bobby" as a kind of death.

Some believe Orr was never whole, that his knees were already banged up when his messianic mission in Boston began. He'd been playing serious hockey against older and bigger kids since he was 12. Milt Schmidt once quipped that if the rules allowed, Orr could have played in the NHL when he was in the eighth grade. He might have been better off. The scorecard on Orr's ruinous knee injuries has always been muddled by the

Hockey laureate Red Fisher of Montreal said of Orr: "Was there ever a player like him before or since he burst on the game like a flaming, runaway comet at the age of 18? With Orr, the show began the instant he hunched over and cradled the puck on the blade of his stick."

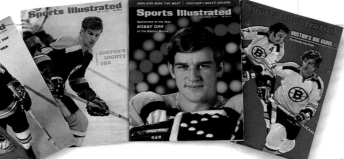

patient's secretiveness, but the surgical process probably started when his right knee was cut for ligament repairs after Orr collided with a teammate in a Winnipeg charity game in the summer of 1967. During the subsequent season, he got cranked by the Leafs' Marcel Pronovost, causing left knee ligament problems that were repaired in the summer of 1968. This is the surgery some armchair orthopedists believe did not go well, leading to all the problems down the road, though it should be noted that Orr came along just before the perfecting of the arthroscopic process that made knee jobs simpler and safer. He was breezing along the next season until he caught his skate in an ice rut at the L.A. Forum. He made it through the season, then had his left knee cut again in the summer of 1969. Three summers; three knee jobs.

There followed almost three full seasons—his best—of no major injuries until he got steamrolled by a Red Wing in March of 1972. While a bad blow, he played through it and had a stupendous playoff, scoring 24 points in 15 games en route to the second and last Cup of his era. But the ache in the left knee was awful, the swelling was alarming, and he was icing it constantly. He knew that this time, it was different. Surgery in the summer of 1972 wired him back together, and he had three more superb seasons, but he was doing it as much with guile and reputation as with the sheer, ungodly skills he once had. And in his heart, he knew something was gone for good. Opponents began to sense it, too. In 1973, Charlie Burns, a cagey old Bruin then playing for the North Stars, noted: "Bobby Orr is not the Orr of old. His knees will not let him be. He used to own the game up and down the ice all night. Now, he picks his spots." Proof of which was doubtless the fact that his points slipped that year from 117 to 101. But the next season he had 122, and then in the 1974–75 season he had, with ravaged knees, what his coach that year, Don Cherry, believes was the greatest season any player ever had: 46 goals, 89 assists, and a plus 128 (league leaders average about 50). These are incomprehensible numbers for a defenseman, let alone one playing on one good leg.

The next season he played only 10 games (scoring 18 points), had the left knee cut twice more, heard his surgeon advise, "you only have a few miles left," engaged the Bruins in the mother of all contract wars, left for the Blackhawks in an ugly showdown orchestrated by his duplicitous agent (who eventually went to jail), and started down an angry road to a bitter retirement two years later at the age of 30 when he might have been at his zenith. It should not have come to that, and the fact that his agent conned him, which was verified in a federal court, was clearly a factor. But so was Orr's stubbornness. He became intransigent when he wrongly concluded that the Bruins were trying to shaft him. The young Orr was as hardheaded as any man I ever knew. Still, it just wasn't fair, and for Orr that was an issue he had a lot of trouble with.

IF Orr had been lucky and healthy enough to play as long as Doug Harvey did, he would have played 15 seasons with Ray Bourque (left). Consider that!

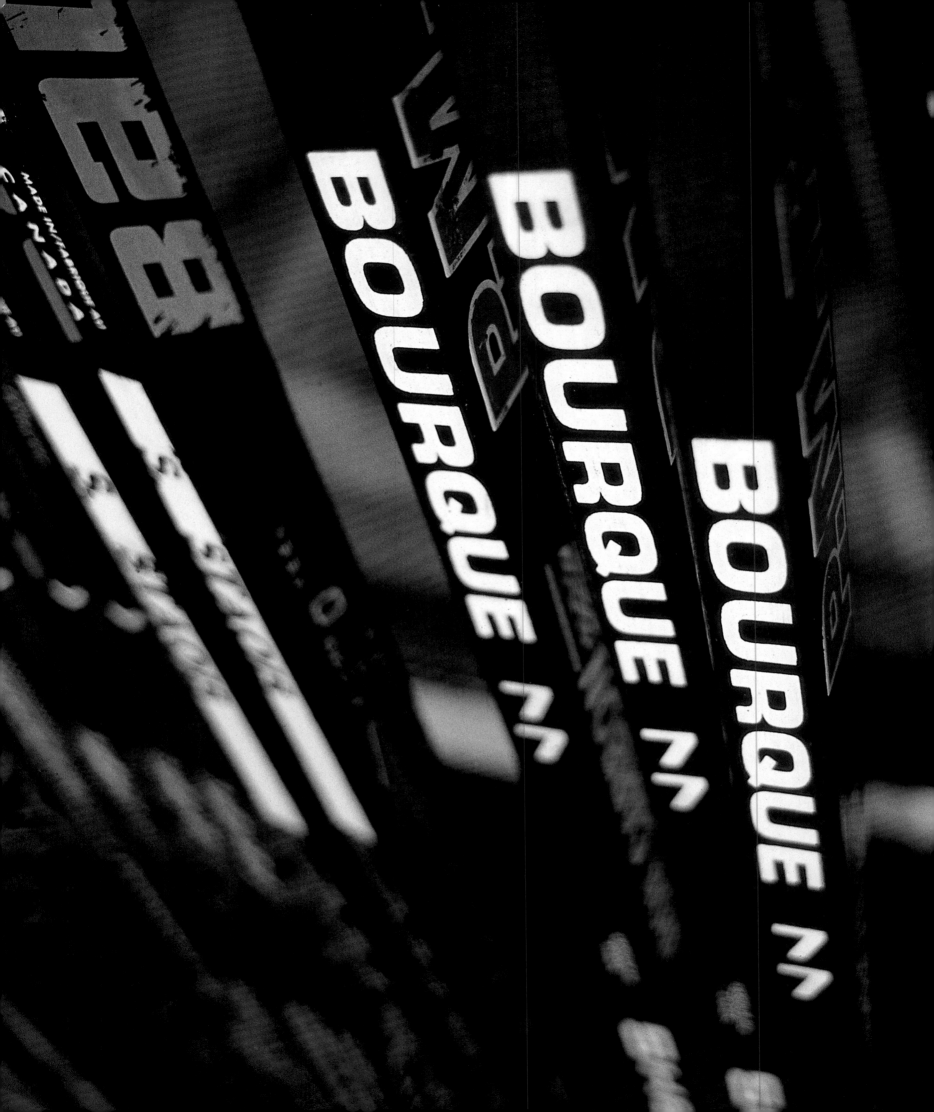

Although in the end, and to his credit, he worked his way through it. The Orr story, given all of its levels of excellence and passion, complexity and melodrama, may be the best sports story of the last 50 years. It could have been a great novel. Only it was all true.

Orr did not break records, he smashed them. He won trophies by the bushel. He was reasonably healthy nine years, and he won the Norris Trophy, for best defenseman, eight times. He set a record for most trophies won in a season: four. When he came into the league, the record for goals by a defenseman was 20. He scored 46. The record for points was 59. He peaked at 139, and six years in a row he scored more than 100 points, which, before he arrived, had never been done by anyone, defenseman or forward. Before he arrived, the record for assists was 59. In the 1970–71 season, he had 102. It was almost absurd how casually he shattered the game's standards. In the history of all sport, only Ruth's assault on the record book was the equivalent of Orr's. Yet, magnificent as the numbers may be, they are dry and dusty compared with the stunning presence he brought to his sport. He was sui generis! Having said that, what more can you say?

RAY BOURQUE

Eddie Shore and Bobby Orr cast such long shadows over Bruins history that it's impossible for anyone to muscle in on their claims to a total eminence. But that has not kept Raymond Bourque from trying for a whole generation. On any other NHL team he'd be an all-time, first team all-star. In Montreal he'd be paired with Doug Harvey; in Toronto with Tim Horton or King Clancy; in Chicago with Pierre Pilote; in Detroit with Red Kelly. You get the point.

But in Boston, Raymond Bourque doesn't have a chance. If he personally delivered a couple of Stanley Cups in the twilight of his career, he might dislodge Eddie Shore. But he could play another century and not seriously threaten the strangle hold Bobby Orr has on Bruins myth and the affections of the team's patrons. Life is unfair. Lou Gehrig languished similarly in the shadow of Babe Ruth, and for most of his career,

Ray Bourque trails only Paul Coffey in career statistics. They are the only defensemen with more than 350 goals, 1,000 assists, and 1,400 points. But Bourque maintained much higher defensive standards while piling up points.

With 40 years in the game, including a decade as a dandy Bruins right winger, Johnny Peirson is a shrewd and candid judge

of NHL talent. Of Ray Bourque, he says: "Bourque has a great sense of how the game is played. He is very quick, has a great

shot, and is masterful at the point. He's a strong skater and very good on his feet. If you watch him move that puck out of

his end, he invariably makes the right pass. His vision is superb."

Mickey Mantle was denied his proper due in New York simply because he had the temerity to not only follow Joe DiMaggio but to play the same position while trying to serve the same purpose. Like Mantle, Bourque didn't choose so thankless a role; he got stuck with it. Unlike Mantle, he never let it bother him.

Only Gordie Howe compares with him in the ranking of the most durable players in the game's history.

Bourque's 1,000th-point puck scored against Washington, February 29, 1992.

Orr had been gone three years and his number 4 had been resting in the Garden rafters five months when the Bruins got Bourque in the 1979 draft. It was a vintage year for defensemen. Nine went in the first round, and Bourque was neither the highest rated nor the Bruins' preference. His junior coach at Verdun always claimed the Bruins never even scouted Bourque. They actually coveted Keith Brown, who would prove to be a nice player lasting 16 years in the league. When the Hawks, choosing one pick ahead of them, took Brown, the Bruins got Bourque by default. So you could call it luck, but as Branch Rickey used to say, "Luck is the residue of design." The only reason they were drafting high enough—eighth overall—to get Bourque was because Harry Sinden had conned Los Angeles into surrendering a first pick for a certain Ron Grahame, a pleasant fellow but ordinary goalie, in one of Harry's most outrageous capers back in the '70s, when he was red-hot in the wheeling and dealing dodge.

If getting Bourque was touched with luck, appreciating what they got was instantaneous. Sinden recalls that on Bourque's first shift at training camp that summer he did something rare, the sort of thing you can't teach, and Harry nudged his pal, the scout Bart Bradley, and said, "Did you see that?" Whereupon, Harry says, they both got goose bumps. Then in his first season, Bourque did something not even Orr did. He not only won the Calder Trophy as Rookie of the Year but he was named to the league's first team all-stars. The bad news was, the invidious comparisons with Orr had only just begun.

In an age in which athletes are seen as feckless hired guns willing to drift wherever the extra buck is dangled, Bourque's loyalty is noteworthy. He is playing out a long career with one team in one town while never demanding top money or making much of an issue of it. His service to the community has been admirable. He's seen as a blue-ribbon family man. There

Bourque spanned the '80s, dominating the decade game in, game out. At the start his supporting cast included Park, Middleton, Milbury, and O'Reilly. In the middle years there were Pederson, Crowder, O'Connell, Fergus, Kluzak, Linseman, and Simmer. At the end there were Neely and Byers, Burridge and Janney, Brickley and Poulin. Early on he defended Pete Peeters in goal; at the end, Lemelin and Moog. During the decade he played for six coaches. The comings and goings were endless. Bourque alone was constant.

From his very first game, right, and season, above, Bourque disdained flamboyance. As a defenseman, he was rarely reckless. "He plays very crafty, much like Doug Harvey," hockey scholar Eddie Sandford observes. "Like Harvey, he doesn't waste his time and energy chasing fellows into the corner or banging them off the boards. But if they're coming down center ice with the puck, he'll bang 'em good!"

have been no scandals or even controversies. His public thinks of him as a throwback, which, while simplistic, is unmistakably high praise. Sinden is his biggest fan. Of no player from any age does the crusty and utterly realistic Bruins boss speak with more feeling. It is more than respect that he has for Bourque. It is affection. Constantly asked to compare Orr and Bourque, Sinden has an answer worthy of Solomon. He says, "If I'm down a goal, I'd want Bobby, but if I'm ahead a goal, I want Ray." It's his way of according Bourque a kind of equality with The Divinity. The endless comparisons, however, irk Sinden. He thinks the quibbling has demeaned Bourque.

But no one quibbles about his skills. His skating, always his strongest suit, remains superior. His sense of the tactics of playing defense are shrewder and smarter than ever. He still has the cannon of a shot from the point, and it's still stunningly accurate. His overall game, which was always remarkably clean, remains so. After 19 seasons, he is still a complete and total force, only marginally less than he was in his prime. The sheer ice time that he gets, which

"If I'm down a goal, I'd want Bobby, but if I'm ahead a goal, I want Ray."

—HARRY SINDEN

was always his most impressive statistic, is still remarkable. Other greats who played as long, like Clapper, Bucyk, Horton, Harvey, Gadsby, Howell, and Delvecchio, became spot and role players in the end. But not Gordie Howe or Wayne Gretzky. And not Raymond Bourque. Playing long and well is the best revenge.

Nearing age 40, Bourque links the game's ages. Jean Ratelle, who played against Rocket Richard, set Bourque up for his first goal in 1979, and now Raymond grooms Joe Thornton, who was three months old the day Bourque scored that goal. Bourque bridges Bruins eras from the afterglow of Don Cherry to the coming of Pat Burns. He has seen it all and done it all except win the Cup and escape the shadow of Orr. If and when he retires, and if he outlasts Paul Coffey, he may be the highest scoring defenseman in history, he will have won the second-most Norris Trophies (second only to you know who), and he will be no worse than second to Howe in total all-star selections. Along the way he has greatly eclipsed all of Orr's career records because, obviously, he has played well more than twice as many games. So, it doesn't count! Right? Bourque can live with that. He always has. He knows he's been lucky and blessed; rather more so than the chap to whom he will always be compared.

THE BRUINS HONORED NUMBERS

It will come as a surprise to the Celtics, who have sometimes uneasily shared quarters with the Bruins for a half century, but the Bruins started retiring numbers and honoring their elect three years before Red Auerbach even came to town, let alone started winning all those titles. The Bruins have been, however, a little more selective than the Celtics in designating their immortals. Merely being a Hall of Famer or a colorful character isn't enough, which is why only seven numbers hang from their rafters. Seven honorees in 75 years suggests the unstated criteria is plenty tough.

Lionel Hitchman's number 3 was the first to be retired. Resolute and imperial, Hitch served off-seasons with the Royal Canadian Mounties, and he looked the part. He was the sort of fellow you'd want next to you in a foxhole. He was the Bruins' first home-grown star, arriving only months after C. F. Adams landed the franchise. He captained the '29 Cup champs and quietly complemented his flamboyant defense partner, Eddie Shore, for nearly a decade. Frank Graham,

the estimable New York scribe, wrote of the pairing: "If you try to go outside them, they'll break your back against the boards." They were fearsome.

Hitch was a pure defenseman. In his entire career, he had 28 goals and 33 assists, which would be meager numbers in a single season for a Ray Bourque. But in Hitchman's case the stats were irrelevant. Shore grabbed headlines with his excesses and brought the masses to their feet with his dazzling rushes, while Hitchman minded the store and protected his goalie, virtues that were more deeply appreciated in those defense-minded times. Bruins fans have always valued character in their players, which is why they

revered Hitch. When he retired in 1934 there was no great fanfare, which was also consistent with the times. But over the years that followed, number 3 got set aside until another Hitchman came along. It never happened.

The first of the great ceremonies honoring a retiree inevitably elevated Aubrey Victor Clapper, known as "Dit" and wearer of the number 5. He was tall, gallant, courtly, and in all the pictures of him with his slicked-back hair and brilliant smile he seems a dead ringer for Gary Cooper when he was young and dashing. Clapper was a matinee idol of a player when people could still believe their jock heroes were a

special breed. He was the first NHL player to last 20 years, the first to skate up to the age of 40, the first to be an all-star as both a defenseman and forward. He was a clean, rather noble player on the ice and the same sort of man off the ice. He was godfather to the Krauts and father figure to a whole generation of Bruins. In 1942, the Leafs' Bingo Kampman skated over his leg, severing his Achilles tendon, but he played five more years. Nor was his courage confined to the rink. Once on a late fall fishing trip he swam a half mile through the icy waters of a Canadian lake to save three companions whose canoe had swamped. That was Dit; just a little larger than life.

The tribute February 2, 1947, was unprecedented. Clapper, who was putting aside his skates to devote himself to coaching the team, was showered with gifts: $2,000 in government bonds from the fans, a handsome silver service from the league, assorted booty from the players, and a plaque from the writers. But what made it most unusual was the fact that not only was Clapper's number

Lionel Hitchman played through agonizing pain, using a specially designed helmet to protect his broken jaw.

retired but he was also, right there on the spot, made a member of the Hockey Hall of Fame. It's the only time a player has gone directly from the ice to the Hall.

It was indefensible, other than on grounds of popularity, but Clapper's number 5 actually got retired before Shore's number 2. Eddie the maverick's departure in 1940 had been stormy. He goaded the Bruins into dumping him by buying an American Hockey League franchise in Springfield, then demanding the right to split his time between the Bruins and his own team. It was

ludicrous. At 37 and having taken a fierce beating for a generation there was no way even a titan like Shore could effectively divide himself between two teams. So they peddled him to the Americans at a nifty profit, where he played only 15 more games. When he got ornery, Shore could drive a deacon to drink. Still, one suspects the Ross-Adams axis was being disingenuous in holding a grudge against Shore, given what he'd meant to the franchise.

Finally, in a modest ceremony before a playoff game two months after the Clapper festival, Shore's number 2, worn with a passion surely not exceeded in the history of sport, was retired. He received a diploma citing his earlier election to the Hall of Fame and a rousing ovation. It was overdue. He'd been gone seven years and in

that time, two lads, Flash Hollett and Pat Egan had been allowed to wear number 2. Both were worthy. But Shore was one of a kind.

Milt Schmidt's number 15 and Johnny "the Chief" Bucyk's number 9 were retired because, like Hitchman and Clapper, both fairly defined the team and its sense of itself. Together, Schmidt and Bucyk span six decades of Bruins history with only the interruption of a war. Both were distinguished by a rare combination of performance and sportsmanship while collectively serving in every capacity save ownership without bringing a single blemish to their team. Schmidt's patriarchal status in Bruins folklore was cemented ages ago, but Bucyk's niche can be undervalued. When he was at his physical peak he played for a lousy team. When the team got good, he was overshadowed by more explosive and colorful comrades. It's instructive that he could not have cared less.

Among hockey people, Bucyk's stature is monumental. He lasted 23 seasons and 1,540

games; only Gordie Howe and Alex Delvecchio played more. Bucyk remains among the all-time leaders in goals, 556, and points, 1,369. And yet stats don't do him justice either, for they don't convey how sound he was in every aspect of play at both ends of the ice while also being indestructible.

Johnny Bucyk

Milt Schmidt's Jersey

Built like a minivan, "the Chief" was more durable than any other player. The subtle works hockey people consider beautiful were his specialty: digging the puck from the corner, tipping shots at the goal mouth, feeding the point-man on the power play, tying up an opponent, delivering thunderous body-checks that were also exquisitely clean, which scholars say he did better than any other winger who ever played the game. That so physical a player could win the Lady Byng Trophy for gentlemanly play twice was astounding as well as a measure of his perfection of basic technique. His disdain for fisticuffs or even marginal rowdiness was legend. Research indicates he was challenged by a certain Marcel Bonin, a rugged and ill-tempered Canadien, back around 1958. Bonin was left in a heap. The Chief played 20 more years without ever again being "challenged."

In terms of theater, the retiring of Phil Esposito's number 7, December 3, 1987, was memorable. Esposito's departure in the landmark trade with the Rangers that brought Brad Park and Jean Ratelle to the Bruins had left bruised sensitivities that took 12 years

to salve. In the meantime, Raymond Bourque had come to town, and had been awarded Esposito's old number, which he'd further distinguished, leaving the Bruins with a dilemma. Pointedly, the actual retiring of the number Bourque was still wearing was not a scheduled event on the program honoring Espo that night.

But Bourque had other ideas. "The decision was made about 1:30 that afternoon," he later recalled. "Very few people knew what was going to happen. Management knew, the training staff, my wife. I actually went into the back room after warm-ups to put the jersey on. So nobody saw me do it." At the ceremony, the overwhelmed Esposito was at center ice surrounded by his chums from the Big Bad Bruins era when Bourque skated over and began to remove his jersey emblazoned with the large 7 and for a long moment there was a hush all over the building until it became clear that Bourque was returning 7 to Esposito and taking for himself a new number, 77. Whereupon, the building erupted. Says Esposito, "I remember looking at him and saying, 'What are you doing?' And he said to

me, 'This is yours, big guy. It's never been mine. It's always been yours and it should always be yours.'"

Inevitably the most melodramatic of the numbers rituals focused on the most dramatic of their performers, Bobby Orr, number 4. By January 1979, almost three years had passed since his bitter departure to Chicago; more than a year had passed since he'd reluctantly submitted to the reality that his knees were shot and he was finished as a player. Orr returned, he

later confessed, against his better judgment. He wondered about lingering resentments, and even if there were none, he wasn't sure he could handle the emotion. On the other hand, Bruins management was fearful that simmering fan anger over Orr's leaving, which had not yet been proven misplaced, might turn the event into a spectacle that could get unpleasant. Everyone was uptight.

Ray Bourque's classy numbers switch leaves Phil Esposito flabbergasted. Equally astounded is Espo's pal, the late and greatly missed Frosty Forristall (center). MC Bob Wilson (right) didn't know it was coming either, but handled it glibly.

All the anxieties dissolved when Orr, in a three-piece brown suit and looking more like an aspiring junior executive than a retired demigod, stepped onto the ice to be engulfed by a tidal wave of sheer affection. Senators, governors, mayors, commissioners, and an awestuck visiting all-star team from the Soviet Union were among the onlookers. But the joy of the moment sprang from the rafters and across the length and breadth of the old Garden, where ordinary people had understood from the start that Orr, the fabulous man-child, had been touched with a talent that was purely divine; so much so, that his season would be necessarily short.

Orr belonged to them and on this evening, they got him back.

The first avalanche of cheering lasted 20 minutes. "You have just broken the GUINNESS BOOK OF RECORDS standard for the longest standing ovation," said the MC, the GLOBE'S Tom Fitzgerald. When he got to speak, Orr said simply: "I spent 10 years in Boston and they were the best years of my life. I love you all!" And again the cheering shook the old building. Then he donned his jersey with the number 4 on the back one last time, and with his wife, Peggy,

alongside, he watched, his lower lip trembling and tears welling, as the emblem with the 4 was lifted to the rafters while the organist played "Auld Lang Syne." There was not a dry eye in the house.

Said Wayne Cashman, who had been his teammate when they were mere boys in Oshawa: "Every night we played he did something either new or better than it had ever been done before and he left me amazed. Every

night." It remained for Don Cherry, then the Bruins coach who had witnessed the surpassing emotion of it all from the bench, to speak to the irony many that night found too difficult to state: "It really tore me apart to watch him pull on that sweater," said Cherry. "All I could think of is what might have been."

On the January night in 1979 that they retired Bobby Orr's number 4 with a thunderous roar, Orr was two months shy of his 31st birthday.

Phil Esposito's 100th Goal Stick

Dit Clapper's Jersey

WICKED BATTLES

CHAPTER FOUR

The personal feuds and tribal vendettas hockey players engage at the drop of an insult dominate the annals of every team, none more so than the Bruins. Hockey is all about intimidation and pain. The game struts courage and loyalty as the highest virtues. Pride is inviolate. Tribal canons supersede common sense. "Tit for tat" is the law of this jungle. For better or worse no team has understood the entire package, in all of its anthropological complexity, more fully than the Bruins, and they have been quick to celebrate exemplars of their governing motif, as they define it.

In contemporary times, the best example was Cam Neely. He was a battleship on skates. In his prime he rolled over everything that strayed into his path. He intimidated opponents by merely climbing over the boards. He was no choirboy, but his good looks and disarming manner charmed the town. He hung out with Michael J. Fox and became the darling of the celebrity culture. If Hollywood had invented hockey, Neely would have been central casting's puck-chasing prototype. He liked the role, but he was no dandy. He

In a terrific moment, Barry Pederson won the draw. Mike Gillis set the screen. And Brad Park, who is at the bottom of this pile, drilled the goal that eliminated Buffalo in sudden death in the '83 Playoffs. In Boston, Park found peace of mind and responded with brilliance. "No one could read the play like Brad Park," says Harry Sinden. He played the game as if it were a round of chess. Sinden robbed the Rangers twice; first when he stole Park and the incomparable Jean Ratelle and later when he swiped Rick "Nifty" Middleton in an even more outrageously one-sided larceny.

understood his fame was vested not in his charms but in his punishing style, not in the clubs but on the ice. Such warriors always attract bitter foes, blood rivals. Neely had plenty. The most colorful was Claude Lemieux. The most lethal was truculent Swede Ulf Samuelsson, who was built like a wolverine and had a similar temperament. Their war lasted a decade spanning brutish Ulfie's stints with the Whalers and the Penguins and most of Neely's career, which Ulfie helped ruin. When they met on the ice, the renewing of their struggle eclipsed the game, as Ulfie sought to kneecap Cam or Cam tried to impale Ulfie on the backboards. The Swede ultimately prevailed because he was a touch more cynical. Without question, the knee and hip trauma that curtailed Neely's brilliant career was aggravated by Samuelsson, who doubtless understood precisely what he was doing. In the simplistic world of sport, where good and evil are defined by the colors of uniforms, Neely was Galahad and Samuelsson was Modred. The issue was honor and the bad guy won. It's an Old Testament game. The sword cuts both ways.

On the other hand, the Bruins have usually been pleased to give more often than receive. Lionel Hitchman and the Montreal Maroons' Hooley Smith had a dandy contempt for one another that persisted like the Neely-Samuelsson feud, year after year. In 1930, Hooley whacked Lionel over the head with his stick while, according to newspaper accounts, the Maroons fans who had been "screaming for Bruins blood all night" chanted "war whoops." Happily, Hitch was wearing an ugly helmet designed by Art Ross, having recently broken his jaw in yet another stick fight with another Maroon. The Bruins-Maroons rivalry got so fierce Ross made his defensemen wear helmets when they met, a full half century before helmets became commonplace. The Hitchman-Smith feud actually began in 1927, when the irascible Hooley was with the Ottawa Senators and cheap-shotted Harry Oliver, breaking his nose. RCMP Sergeant Hitchman, who took his Bruins captaincy very seriously, was having a late snack in a nearby saloon after the game when who should walk in but Hooley. Hitch sprang from his stool, dumped the meal, and took after Hooley, and they were last seen racing down a darkened Ottawa street in the dead of night.

The infamous Shore-Bailey incident

On December 12, 1933, Eddie Shore bushwhacked Toronto's Ace Bailey at the Boston Garden, almost killing him. The incident branded Shore a historical villain and cemented his game's violent image. It was a heavy price for a moment's caprice. Shore regretted it. But he never apologized.

The Bruins and Leafs had a mutual loathing that stemmed from the ancient feud of their leaders, Art Ross and Connie Smythe. Early on that night there were four vicious brawls. Dit Clapper and King Clancy fought. So did Shore and Red Horner. A newspaper reported, "The Garden ice was soaked with Shore's blood. He had taken a terrible beating from the Toronto sticks while aiding goalie Thompson." With nerves frazzled and the Bruins holding a two-man advantage, Smythe sent out his rowdies, Horner and Clancy, along with the classy Bailey to kill the penalties.

A clever stick-handler, Ace thwarted two of Shore's forays, and "the

Edmonton Express" was frustrated as he curled the net and thundered up ice in one of his signature rushes that always lifted the crowd from their seats. But along the boards, Shore got crunched, not by the hated Horner—as he always claimed—but by the impish Clancy. Shore hit the boards headfirst and lay crumpled on the ice for a few seconds. Emerging from his daze in a terrible fury, he charged the nearest Leaf, crashed him at full speed, cross-checking him just above the kidneys, and flipping him into the air. It just happened to be the innocent Bailey, and when he landed on his head the impact could be heard all over the ice. Smythe's assistant, Frank Selke, Jr., later wrote: "Bailey was laying on the blue line with his head turned sideways as though his neck was broken. His knees were raised, legs twitching ominously. Suddenly a hush fell over the Arena. Everyone realized Bailey was badly hurt."

It got supremely ugly. An enraged Horner turned on Shore and dropped him with an uppercut. Selke added: "When he fell, his body rigid as a board, Shore's head struck the ice splitting open and in an instant, he was circled by a pool of blood three feet in diameter." Bruins players hurdled the dasher and charged Horner, but Charlie Conacher lined up next to Red, and with the two of them holding their sticks like bayonets, Conacher snarled, "Which of you guys is going to be the first to get it." Doctors labored over Bailey on the ice for 19 minutes. When they got him to the dressing room he was turning blue, and Dr. Martin Crotty, a Holy Cross man who was the Bruins' physician, said, "Find out if the boy is a Catholic because if he is, we need a priest to give him the last rites of the Church right now."

Bailey had a double skull fracture. It was nip and tuck for two weeks, but he made it. Suspended 16 games, Shore took off for the Caribbean, which offended many. Bailey's career was finished, but two months later he was able to attend a Toronto all-star game, which raised $17,000 for his family. Looking old and wearing dark glasses, Ace walked gingerly onto the ice, and when he reached Shore he embraced him amidst a deafening tumult. "It wasn't his fault," Bailey said. "We just didn't see each other coming."

This determined disdain for the turning of the other cheek, which became quite genetic, was the quality Ross demanded from the get-go. Trumpeting the 1926 squad, the GLOBE declared, "They are a fighting, snarling team that will take nobody's backwash this season." Nor did they take anyone's "backwash" the next season, nor the next. "Battles" have greater prominence in their history than most teams, although many of their great rumbles have been

> "They are a fighting, snarling team that will take nobody's back-wash this season."

more farcical than mean.

Take the notorious Christmas Night donnybrook with the aptly named Philadelphia Quakers in 1930. Harvard man George Owen started it by decking the Quakers' Hib Milks, and it got so far out of hand that overwhelmed Garden police considered calling in the marines stationed at nearby Charlestown Navy Yard. When the Bruins' Marty Barry pounded on Gerry Lowery in the evening's last joust, the organist played "Silent Night." It was hilarious. There was a sequel during Christmas week 47 years later at Madison Square Garden when Mike Milbury, Terry O'Reilly, and the usually pastoral Peter McNab climbed into the seats and tangled with abusive Rangers fans. At the height of the fiasco, Milbury—the thoughtful Colgate grad—whaled on one 300-pound heckler with the fan's own shoe, then scaled it across the ice. It was pure SLAP SHOT! An even zanier slice of "old-time hockey" came in a blooming 1977 exhibition game in Philadelphia when a fight between Wayne Cashman and the Flyers' Jim Watson spread from the aisles to the seats, to the corridors, and finally to the bowels of the Spectrum. George Plimpton was there, and his account in his superb Bruins book OPEN NET is terrific. John Wensink, the most likeable of the goons, challenged the entire North Star bench one evening in 1978. It was truly Homeric. Three years later, when Wensink was safely retired, Minnesota got even by provoking a pier sixer that resulted in 401 penalty minutes, the NHL record. Briefly it was feared Gentleman Jean Ratelle might be the only Bruin not in the Sin Bin and would have to face the North Stars all by himself.

Rather less amusing were the more personal vendettas. Old-timers say a 1951 stick fight between the Bruins' "Wild" Bill Ezinicki and the Red Wings' immortal "Terrible Ted" Lindsay was the cruelest. Lindsay sliced Ezinicki for 19 stitches plus a broken nose. After the game, Lindsay raced to the first-aid room where Ezinicki was being sewn. "Are you all right?" Terrible Ted asked. "I'm all right," Wild Bill replied. And that was the end of it. But by 1975 times had changed, and when Dave Forbes, an intense Bruins' winger, clubbed Minnesota's Henry Boucha over the head with his stick, there was hell to pay. The incident haunted Forbes and shortened his career. Later in life, he turned to religion.

During their heyday, the Big Bad Bruins of the Orr era battled everyone and trashed all the conventions, offending even hardened hockey men. "They are out and out lawless," Frank Selke, Jr., once lamented. "I don't even

Following spread: **A**ll in a night's work, the contemporary Bruins hassle with the Sabres with Rob Dimaio (19) stirring it up. Instigating tiffs is an art form. The Bruins' best were the equally infuriating Leo Labine, John McKenzie, and Ken Linseman. DiMaio might be in their class if the times allowed it.

think they know the rules," Hawks coach Billy Reay added. "It's like mayhem to play in Boston." All of which only

amused the saucy Bruins, but their "attitude" often did get out of hand. An example was a vicious stick duel between Eddie Shack and the NHL's only Jewish player, the Flyers' Larry Zeidel, who charged that certain Bruins had goaded him with ethnic slurs and wisecracks. Far from denying it, a Bruins official defended the antics by noting that Zeidel had called Phil Esposito "a Wop." They were skating on thin ice. It almost seemed the tragedy of Ted Green in a pointless exhibition game in 1969 was the inevitable consequence of a belligerence gone awry. Green was as fierce and fearless as any man who ever laced on skates; "a man of sanctified savagery" is what Chris Lydon called him. He terrorized opponents. In

*F*or a decade Milt Schmidt (center) and "Black Jack" Stewart (not shown) waged a fierce, often bloody, feud without ever realizing why it even began.

1964, the owner of the Rangers actually put a bounty on his head. But in a dumb fracas with Wayne Maki, a manic little Blues journeyman, he nearly lost his life when Maki, scared out of his wits, struck him on the temple with his stick, fracturing his skull. "After that I was so much scrambled eggs" was the arresting way Green put it. He eventually came back. But he was no longer "Terrible Ted."

On the level of art, the Bruins' greatest battles have been with Montreal. Testimony to that runs throughout these pages. When the Maroons went out of business in 1938, the Canadiens gladly picked up the cudgel. Second in the ranks of their archfoes over these 75 years are the Rangers. The last time they met for the Cup, 1972, was a barn-burner crowned by a monumental irony. Brad Park, the Rangers' mainstay, had infuriated the "Big Bads" with some snippy remarks in a book he'd coauthored. Their contempt for him was chilling, even spilling over into the annual all-star game. "I hated even sharing the dressing room with that creep Park," the ever-diplomatic John McKenzie snarled. "His presence took all the joy out of being an All-Star." In the playoffs, the Bruins seemed as intent on destroying Park as winning the Cup. McKenzie, Wayne Cashman, Don Awrey, Ace Bailey, and Derek Sanderson took turns running and carving him every time he touched the puck. But Park never let up, never backed down, and never whined. Three years later, after the "Big Bad" era crashed, Park came to Boston and, in the opinion of Harry Sinden, bailed out the franchise.

Third of the archfoes are the Maple Leafs. Their nasty relationship crested in the opening game of the '69 Playoffs in a scene Milt Schmidt called the scariest he ever saw in hockey. The Bruins were rolling 6–0 when Bobby

*I*n a vintage pose, the routinely menacing Wayne Cashman has his stick aimed at the throat of the Canucks' Harold Snepsts. When Wayne got really mad, his eyes tilted. Ranking the all-time scariest Bruins, "Terrible Ted" Green is third, Bob "Dr. Hook" Schmautz is second, and "Cash" wins the prize.

Don Quixote on skates, Terry O'Reilly, makes the Canadiens' Yvon Lambert pay for his sins. No sane player ever tried to go

through O'Reilly, and it was less advisable to ram between him and the boards. Nobody in sports worked harder to perfect

his skills. But his work ethic could get eerie, and the Irish temper was a sight to behold. A perfect gentleman off ice, he spent

his time on the road studying math books and searching for antiques. Terry was deep.

Orr, who had been floating sublimely all night doing what he darn well pleased, came roaring along the right wing boards and made the mistake of dropping his head just as Pat Quinn stepped into his path. Quinn wasn't greatly skilled but he was as tough as his name. He decked Orr with a thunderous and perfectly legal check. Orr crumpled like a rag doll and fell on his face, and when he didn't move for a few seconds, the Garden erupted. As fights raged all over the ice, 15,000 people screeched over and over, "Get Quinn . . . Get Quinn." History's largest lynch mob seemed to be forming. Orr was lugged to a nearby hospital. In the third period, rumors that Orr was unconscious and in surgery swept the building. Then the Leafs' Forbes Kennedy, a nutty little ex-Bruin, got into a stick fight with Gerry Cheevers, sparking a new round of brawls. I left the press box and circled the first balcony and was stunned by the rage. Wrote Toronto columnist George Gross: "Boston Garden turned into a lunatic bin. The only thing missing was the straightjackets." He was right. The place was a cauldron. The Leafs needed a police escort to get out of the building. Orr starred in the next game and the Bruins swept the series.

If all Bruins coaches warred with officials, Art Ross took the prize. Infuriated by the officiating in the 1927 Finals, Ross posted a $500 bounty. Wild Billy Coutu, above, accepted, chased down the ref, punched him out, collected the $500, and got banished from hockey for life. Ross went unpunished. Following Spread: Bruins dogma holds that a well timed rumble can be therapeutic. This early '60s dance in the fog is with the Canadiens.

But the great battles are not always about riot and rage. They are as much laden with humor as hate. The Bruins-Leafs rivalry mirrored the 25-year feud of their outsized mentors, Art Ross and Conn Smythe, two of sports' greatest characters. The flamboyant Smythe, a British colonialist at heart who liked being called "the Major," delighted in rattling Ross's cage. He once bought a huge ad in Boston newspapers mocking the Bruins style as "boring." Ross, calling him "the big wind from Lake Ontario," demanded a fine. But league officials ignored him. Chagrined, Ross is said to have planted two Boston longshoremen next to Toronto's bench to goad Smythe into a fight. It didn't work. Conn came back with a gem. As a rebuke to the sartorial standards of Boston, which he considered inferior, he took to wearing a tuxedo for Bruins games and strutted about like an Edwardian fop tipping his top hat to irate Bruins fans. It was his practice to climb up on the boards to berate the officials. One night he lost his balance and landed in the lap of a lady in the front row, providing Ross—the dour Scot—with a rare guffaw. But the Major was tough to top. On the Leafs' next visit he had Red Horner, his captain, skate over to the lady's box and present her with a bouquet of roses. Another time, when he learned Ross was suffering from "lower GI problems," he had his resident rascal, King Clancy, skate to the Bruins bench with another bouquet along with a note telling Ross precisely where he could "stick" the flowers. But above all the Major was a patriot, a decorated veteran of both world wars. When the two sons of Art Ross got shipped overseas to fight in World War II, Smythe is rumored to have said: "Anybody who could rear two sons like that must be all right." End of feud!

PLAYING TO WIN

CHAPTER FIVE

The Kraut line—Woody (14), Miltie (15), and Bobby (17)—swarm the Leafs' Turk Broda in prewar Stanley Cup combat. As hockey's Rover Boys, they graced the game with their spirited play and ethical manner. Clarence Campbell said of Schmidt: "He typifies everything a hockey player should be."

Opening night of the 1926–27 season, Owner C. F. Adams jauntily posed with his team's two new mascots, a pair of lively brown bears tugging at their chains, while Art Ross and his rugged band looked on. If Adams and Ross seemed humorless, they had a sharp sense of sporting theater. The nightly custom was to introduce the players numerically; each player skated slowly into the rink traced by a spotlight. "It was thrilling," Clif Keane recalls. "On they would come, number 1 Thompson, number 3 Hitchman, number 5 Clapper, on and on while the organist played 'Paree.' Nobody could figure why that was their theme song, but what did it matter." Even grim Eddie Shore was shamelessly used in the hype. Devilishly rakish in a matador's cape and top hat, Shore glided onto the ice aided by a valet, who would remove his cloak while a brass band played "Hail to the Chief" and the crowd went nuts. Surprisingly, Shore enjoyed the nonsense until the New York Americans put a stop to it. They came out one night with a rolled-up carpet, and when it unraveled, out popped tiny winger Rabbit McVeigh, who danced around the rink blowing kisses to the crowd while Shore glowered. Shore never again staged a theatrical entrance.

The cocky antics played well because the early Bruins were very good; Cup finalists their third season, champs their fifth, and in their sixth, they tore the record book to shreds. Their 1929–30 record was 38–5–1, best in NHL history. Ten players went on to the Hall of Fame. The "Dynamite line" of Dit Clapper–Cooney Weiland–Dutch Gainor scored 102 goals. The second, so-called Thunderbolt line, of Harry Oliver-Marty Barry–Perk Galbraith was almost as good. Shore, Lionel Hitchman, and goalie Tiny Thompson were at their peak. Yet the Montreal Canadiens with Howie Morenz, Aurel Joliat, and Johnny "Black Cat" Gagnon blanked them in the playoffs; they did it again the next year on Wilder LaRochelle's goal in sudden death. A pattern was evolving. The '30s were paradoxical. Shore won four MVPs. Thompson won four Vezinas. Ross imported certified legends Nels Stewart, Hooley Smith, Babe Siebert, and Johnny Gagnon. Attendance at the height of the Depression was phenomenal. But from 1930 to 1938, the Bruins did not once reach the Stanley Cup finals.

The spoked B emblem marked their 25th year (1949). (L–R) Ed Harrison was Ed Sandford's cousin. Paul Ronty had multiple 20-goal seasons skating with Johnny Peirson. Clever Jack Crawford served 12 years. Wartime pilot Murray Henderson came from the Conacher clan.

It was the Krauts who changed all that. Milt Schmidt, Woody Dumart, and Bobby Bauer grew up in a Southern Ontario enclave famous for its gritty German stock. Kitchener, Milt and Woody's hometown, was called Berlin until World War I German phobia forced its renaming to honor a warmongering British jingoist. Woody was 13 and Milt 12 when they teamed up on the Kitchener Junior "Greenshirts." Three years later, Bobby, the eldest, came over from Waterloo, the next town, and they were joined as a line for eternity. Two years later, 1935, they reported to the Bruins. By 1937, they were budding stars already famed as "the Krauts," three sturdy, too-good-to-be-true lads who played the game beautifully and honorably. They were genuine Musketeers, doing everything together. They played hockey together all winter, played softball together all summer, negotiated their contracts together, lived at Ma Pearl Snow's Brookline boarding house together, had pregame meals and postgame snacks together, won and lost together, went to war together. "We never got mad at each other because at least we had brains enough to listen to one another," says Schmidt.

"Did you ever have an argument?" I once asked Woody. He thought a moment and said, "I'm not sure. Maybe in

grammar school." Only marriage, after the war, could break them up. But then Milt and Marie Schmidt lived across the street from Woody and Phyllis Dumart almost 30 years, and they now live only about five miles apart. Pressured by his in-laws, Bobby quit after his best season in 1947 to run the family's prestigious skating equipment company. "He quit too soon," says Woody. And he died too soon as well, in 1964 at only 49—killed, his pals believe, by stress. "Bobby worked all hours of the day and there he was still working often in the wee hours of the morning, and he never did get that nice job in the front office he was promised," says Milt rather ruefully. "All the Bauer boys had bad hearts," Woody adds. "All six died young." Some 35 years later the bond is still strong. The Krauts were the physical and spiritual mainstays of the grand team that won two Cups and would have won more save for the war. Yet all that somehow made the story of hockey's noble Musketeers even better.

The Bruins remained potent during World War II thanks to the prodigious scoring of Bill Cowley and Herb Cain. Their fine nucleus included the Jacksons, Flash Hollett, Jack Crawford, Pat Egan, and the flashy teens Bep Guidolin, Ken Smith, and Don Gallinger. Holding it together was the constant Dit Clapper. When the war ended, Ross made him coach and waited for the restoration. But it didn't come. Trounced in the '46 Finals by the Rocket Richard–Elmer Lach–Bill Durnan Canadiens' wagon, Ross, his eyesight fading along with his legendary resolve, had to face rebuilding. Within a year, Roy Conacher was traded while Bauer, Cowley, and Terry Reardon chose retirement. In 1948, the great Brimsek was gone, traded to the Hawks when Ross concluded Mr. Zero had left his legs on a Coast Guard cutter. Then, in a blow that devastated Ross, Gallinger was banished for gambling. Some of the new talent was superior. Johnny Peirson, Eddie Sandford, and Fernie Flaman became quintessential Bruins while Dave Creighton, Paul Ronty, and Pete Babando were worthy. A smart trade with Detroit landed stylish Bill Quackenbush, a future Hall of Famer. But it was a team no longer greatly feared. After three more swift playoff exits, Clapper quit, simply walking away after the 1949 team dinner. "It hit me like a wet towel," said Walter Brown, who was about to become team president. Ross, plainly slipping, replaced Dit with George Boucher, a bush leaguer. "It was a terrible mistake," says Johnny Peirson. Boucher lasted only one stormy season. In a horrible trade they handed Flaman to the Leafs. In 1950, they missed the playoffs. The farm system was in ruins. Attendance dipped under six thousand a game. The team was broke. In 1951 Brown had to borrow from the B & M Railroad to finance operations. In 1952, the Leafs, out of pity, gave them Fleming Mackell to atone for the theft of Flaman. Times were tough when you became dependent on Conn Smythe's charity.

The NHL's only gambling scandal ruined Don Gallinger, once a Bruins teen phenom. Gally and high-scoring Billy Taylor were charged with placing bets against their own team with a Detroit bookie. Both were banished, leaving Gallinger embittered. Ed Sandford says Art Ross was still brooding about the incident on his deathbed.

Don Gallinger

The 1941 champs! Dit Clapper and Milt Schmidt flank Coach Cooney Weiland. 2nd row: Bobby Bauer, "Flash" Hollett, Des Smith, Art Jackson. 3rd row: Pat McCreavy, Woody Dumart, Terry Reardon, Eddie Wiseman, Herb Cain. Far right, Roy Conacher (9) is partially obscured by G.M. Art Ross who is congratulating his lads while puffing on an Old Gold cigarette. They had just come off the ice after rolling to the Cup. Experts were calling them the finest team in hockey history. Seven months later, Japan bombed Pearl Harbor. One year later, eight members of the team were in military uniforms. There would be no more Cups for 29 years.

Many say Terry Sawchuk was the NHL's greatest goalie. By age 25, he'd won three Cups for Detroit when Boston got him in

a nine-player deal in 1955. But for all his skills, Sawchuk was mercurial and haunted. "He was a loner and a drinker and always

complaining," Leo Monahan, who covered him, recalls. "He was not a happy guy, but then goalies can be strange." Late in his

second Bruins season, Sawchuk declared he had mononucleosis, then a new malady. "Hell. We didn't even know how to spell

it," says Monahan. When the press panned him, he threatened a massive libel suit. Lynn Patrick ended the farce by trading him

back to the Red Wings for an unproven prospect, John Bucyk. Sawchuk went on being brilliant but troubled. In 1970, a night's

drinking led to a 3 A.M. brawl with an old "pal," ex-Bruin Ron Stewart. Three weeks later, Sawchuk died. He was 40.

Improbably, they were rescued by a New York Rangers' immortal. Lynn Patrick, son of Lester and brother of Muzz, followed Boucher, then took complete control in 1953 as the worn-out Ross finally stepped aside. Patrick is the quiet man of Bruins history. But the respect he commanded was huge. "Lynn Patrick had a fantastic hockey mind," says Peirson. "He knew players and how to handle them and he was never afraid to change a system or take a chance."

Patrick, aided by Schmidt, whom he made coach in 1954, juggled, conned, and cajoled the outgunned Bruins into eight playoffs and three trips to the finals from 1951 through 1959, albeit five times with losing records. New talent was sparse, but he made the most of it. Doug Mohns became a great player. Don McKenney was superior offensively. Real Chevrefils had rare skills until booze killed him. Leo Labine was a classic Bruins gonzo: a little nutty, but lovable. Bob Armstrong and Warren Godfrey were solid defensemen. Smart deals brought back Flaman, Leo Boivin, and the irrepressible Jerry Toppazzini. Goaltending was a challenge. But Patrick got three fine seasons from a resurrected Sugar Jim Henry, rolled the dice on the brilliant Terry Sawchuk, and after Terry cracked up, rescued Don "Dippy" Simmons from the scrap heap and revived Harry "Apple Cheeks" Lumley. In the Sawchuk deals, he stole Johnny Bucyk and Vic Stasiuk from the Red Wings, then completed the "Uke line" by plucking Bronco Horvath from the Canadiens for peanuts. Patrick's adroit finessing postponed the Bruins' collapse a decade. His teams were tough and honest. The fans came back.

Leo Boivin was a textbook body-checker, maybe the best at the lost art of hip-checking. Leo was one of two premier defensemen the Bruins let get away and then recovered from Toronto in the '50s. The other was the even more rugged Fernie Flaman. Both are Hall of Famers.

It was in these years that "the Canadiens Curse" became the Bruins obsession. Six times—'52, '53, '54, '55, '57 and '58—Boston fought Montreal in the playoffs for the Cup and got thrashed. Their record was an appalling 8–24. In 1952, they had Montreal down a game and behind by two goals in game six on home ice. All they had to do was hang on to get to the finals. But with time running out and down by one, Boom Boom Geoffrion tied it. "He came out of his own end down through center ice, looking both ways but there was no one for him to pass to because we had every-one covered so well," a still-chagrined Eddie Sandford recalls. "So Boomer simply let go with a wicked wrist shot, six inches off the ice, and it caught the corner by the left post. Tie game!" Late in the second overtime, with most of the combatants near exhaustion, obscure reserve Paul Masnick tapped in the winner out of a scrum in front. Galling! En route, goalie Jim Henry took a shot by Doug Harvey right between the eyes. Sandford recalls: "On the train back to Montreal there was a big debate about whether Sugar Jim could play. Both of his eyes were swollen and black. But by game time they'd opened up enough for him to see." Game seven was a gem. Tied in the second period, the manic

Labine leveled Rocket Richard in front of Montreal's bench, catching him on the side of the head with his knee and knocking him cold. "I knew he wasn't mortally wounded," says Sandford. "But I didn't think he'd be back that soon. 'My God,' I thought. 'We have a chance.'" Always most dangerous at dramatic moments, Richard came back as soon as he woke up. "I didn't know where I was or what team I was playing or which end was which," he claims. "But I wanted to finish the game." He also finished Boston with what's been called his greatest goal. Rocket has no memory of it, but Sandford remembers it all too well. "Doug Harvey had the puck deep in their end. They were changing lines. Rocket came on and Doug hit him with a great pass in full flight, and Rocket streaked down the right wing boards, dramatically cut to the left around Bill Quackenbush, and dumped it past Sugar. It was a great, great goal." As the crowd saluted him, the Rocket staggered to his bench and fainted.

"It was a great, great goal." As the crowd saluted him the Rocket staggered to his bench and fainted.

The next year in the playoffs they stunned a fabulous Detroit team featuring Red Kelly, Terry Sawchuk, and the fabled Howe-Abel-Lindsay "Production line." Patrick's strategy was to have Schmidt, Dumart, and Joe Klukay shadow Gordie and his playmates. "If Ted Lindsay goes out for a cup of coffee, I want somebody right out there with him," said Patrick. It was a task made for the old warriors Schmidt and Dumart. They suffocated the Wings stars with relentless checking while the Sandford-Peirson-Fleming Mackell line handled the offense, scoring 15 goals. When Detroit fell in six, it

was termed the biggest upset in NHL history. But waiting for them in the finals were the Flying Frenchmen, and when Sugar Jim went down, it was over. Elmer Lach ended it with a goal that broke up a scoreless beauty in overtime. So the Bruins had to watch Rocket, Elmer, Boom Boom, and the boys waltz the Cup around the Forum, always a Wagnerian sporting moment. "We were very decent in those years, but we were always two or three superstars short of matching them," says Peirson. It was always so bloody frustrating. After one of the evictions, Sandford and Hal Laycoe, the Rocket's historical nemesis, went to eat in a Montreal restaurant. Sandford recalls: "We ordered some food and it was delivered and neither of us was saying much. Finally Laycoe says, 'The hell with this!' And he stands up, turns the table upside-down, and walks out the door. Stuff is everywhere on the floor; a real mess. Waiters come running bringing the bill and I'm still sitting there. So I have to pay for it all, and I don't even drink."

Bruins teams of the 1950s couldn't match the depth of the three super powers of the "Original Six": Toronto, Montreal, and Detroit. But few teams of any era had as many true sporting gentleman. Left to right are Woody Dumart, Lorne Ferguson, Johnny Peirson, and Eddie Sandford, and far right, Milt Schmidt, who became Bruins coach on Christmas Day, 1954. Dumart, Schmidt, Peirson, and Sandford had dignified careers, conducted themselves with class throughout, and continued to serve their team and their community for decades thereafter while maintaining personal standards of eminent civility. When you speak of men being "a credit to their game," you are speaking of Dumart, Schmidt, Peirson, and Sandford.

HARRY SINDEN

Harry Sinden has been a Bruin more than three decades. He's direct and candid the way hockey men think they should be. He's too proud to curry media who don't understand his game or to respond to media bullies who have—from a safe distance—used him as a punching bag. He's an easy guy to underestimate because he disdains

he'd sneer at that, having never wanted to be seen as anything but a "good hockey man." In Canada, he will always have that honor because of his works in 1958 and 1972 when hockey and patriotism were, for Canadians, inextricably linked.

Devoted to the game since childhood, Sinden climbed the amateur

leagues. It meant long shifts at the plant followed by long bus rides, tough games, more long bus rides, and after a couple of hours sleep, back to another shift at the plant—all while starting a family. It wasn't easy. But Sinden was smart, steady, and mature. Important hockey men took notice.

In 1958, he was the 26-year-old

invasion of Hungary; two years since they'd unseated Canada as global hockey kings at the '56 Olympics. Which was the graver offense was, to Canadians, a toss-up. The day of the Oslo showdown, the Dunlops received thousands of telegrams from back home, including one from Prime Minister John Diefenbaker. "It was a long

playing any sort of role. As the Apostle Paul would say, he is what he is, and is comfortable with that, which doubtless rankles his critics even more. Most remarkable is the gap between the huge respect Sinden enjoys within his game and the lesser acclaim he gets in his own backyard. It is the old "prophet's syndrome" at work, although

ranks, and met his wife to be, Eleanor, while playing Juniors at Oshawa. When they married, he had a choice: pursue his hockey dreams or get a job. He decided he lacked both the size and speed to make the NHL, so he went to work as an engineer at a Toronto General Motors plant while moonlighting in the intense senior amateur hockey

captain of the Whitby Dunlops. When they won the prestigious Allan Cup, they got to represent Canada at the World Championships in Oslo. "It was a huge, huge event in the minds of the entire population of Canada because the hatred between the Soviets and the West had become really heavy," Sinden recalls. It was only a year after the Soviet

time ago, but Canadians still remember exactly where they were that day. It was one of those events." They beat the Soviets, 4–2, and Captain Sinden led his team home to a hero's welcome in city after city across Canada.

Two years later, his Canadian Olympic team was beaten by the United States in the Squaw Valley "Miracle on

Ice." "It was the most disappointing thing that ever happened to me in hockey," Sinden says. "We had a great, great, great, team, and the only game we lost out of 35 we played cost us the gold medal. It was brutal." At 28, his playing days were over. Lynn Patrick recruited him for the Bruins, starting him in the low minors on a sure path that led in five years to becoming the coach in Boston. Patrick was his mentor and father figure. "Lynn was brilliant and a lot of fun. I admired him greatly but he was probably just too nice to everybody." And then Harry paused before adding sheepishly, "You know, you really have to be a bit of an ass to do what I do for a living. Honest to God. You have to do things you don't want to do. But you just gotta do them."

In an interesting irony, given that he's now famed for his own fiscal caution and hard bargaining, In 1970, Harry was driven away at the moment of his greatest triumph in a feud over money. When he delivered the Cup in his fourth season in Boston, he was being paid a woeful $17,500. "When we won, I tried to find out what other coaches were making, and I learned those who were having success were making between 25 and 30,000, so I asked for 25." It was a narrow game dominated by tight-fisted owners, none more so than the Adams family. "They offered me 19." In the meantime, a boyhood pal who was a pioneer in the modular home industry offered him $42,000 per year plus a million dollars in stock options to jump to private industry. Harry and Eleanor had by now four daughters. It looked like a pot of gold. But he was a hockey man. A face-saving grand or two would have pacified them. "So, I came back and told them I had an opportunity to leave and make an awful lot of money, and Mr. Adams says, 'Well, Harry, I really hope you enjoy your new career.' I mean this is like two days after we won the Stanley Cup. I thought he might at least say, 'Oh, Harry, we'll give you a little bit more.' No way. He just called my bluff and I could only gulp. I can't even remember how I responded, but as soon as I got out of the office I started crying. Walking through the Garden, I ran into Zibby from the Bull Gang and he said, 'What are you crying about?.' And I said, 'I just quit!' I couldn't believe it."

Neither did the town nor the Game, but Adams could not have cared less. The Sindens' departure occasioned the year's best social event—a Gatsby-esque, lawn party on a lovely August evening tossed by the late sports barrister Bob Woolf. It was elegant. Harry's business twirl was a disaster. In two years his pal bankrupted, leaving the Sindens broke. Yet Harry contends it was a valuable experience. As further proof that the hockey gods indeed work in mysterious ways, the company's collapse freed him in 1972 to coach Team Canada in the first and best of the epic hockey summits with the USSR. When Sinden's all-stars stormed back to win three straight games by one goal in Moscow to take the series 4–3–1, his cult hero status in his homeland was secured for all time. The Bruins promptly welcomed him back as general manager for a lot more than they'd refused to pay two years earlier. He's been in charge ever since, and in the highest councils of the game, he's considered the wisest of the elders. But the status he deserves in his adopted hometown still eludes him.

Harry Sinden as a player in 1966.

Trips to the finals under Schmidt in 1957 and 1958 and drubbings by the Habs punctuated the era. The high-scoring Ukranian or "Uke" line, of Bucyk-Horvath-Stasiuk, all having ancestral roots in Eastern Europe, had a decided Cold War appeal. In 1958–59 they finished second but got whacked by the Leafs in the semis. The next season, they finished fifth, and the next five years they were last. In 1965–66. they inched up to fifth only to slide back into the cellar in 1966–67, the year both Harry Sinden and Bobby Orr arrived. These were the Wilderness years. But they weren't as wretched as legend holds. They had characters you could care about. The Ukes gave way to the artful BOW line of Bucyk, Murray Oliver, and Tommy Williams, the fancy skating American pioneer. The valor of Eddie Johnston, one of the last of the unmasked goalies, was beyond question. Distinguished veterans lent a little class to the losing: Leo Boivin, Tom Johnson, Doug Mohns, Dean Prentice, Andy Hebenton, Charlie Burns (who played with a plate in his head), Don McKenney (scapegoat of the Gallery Gods), and dauntless Jerry Toppazzini were examples. Small as well as old, they often got roughed up. Vivid is the memory of Gordie Howe ending Billy Knibbs' career with a vicious, flagrant spearing. Tom Johnson, star of the Canadiens' '50s dynasty, had his career terminated frightfully one night when the Hawks' Chico Maki slashed his Achilles with his skate. It was deliberate and vile. "Maki was mad about something or other," the laconic Johnson recalls. "The League asked me if I wanted to file a complaint. I told them, 'forget it.'" The Bruins were last in the NHL, but they didn't whine. That pleased their fans. So did the fact that with fearsome Ted Green, Orland "the Marquis of Queensbury" Kurtenbach, and zanies like Forbes Kennedy and "Cement Head" Fleming on the roster, they didn't lose as many fights as games. To the amazement of the sports world, they vastly outdrew the Celtics, who won the championship in basketball every year that the Bruins finished last in hockey.

Meanwhile, the penitential wait for the promised messiah, which began when Bobby Orr was 12, proceeded with an odd assurance that almost justified all the losing. By now, Weston Adams, Sr., son of founder C. F., was back in charge after a 13-year sabbatical on the stock market, during which he let Walter Brown be president. Adams returned with an evangelistic fury, scouting hockey's remote hustings for talent, much to the amusement of real hockeymen. "He was a millionaire who wanted to

be a scout and we were scouts who wanted to be millionaires," said the irrepressible Wren Blair. It got rocky. Patrick was dumped in 1965, replaced by the tyrannical Hap Emms, who almost destroyed the franchise. But in 1966, Harry Sinden, boyish hero of Canada's intense amateur hockey wars, became coach. He was Patrick's fond protégé, and he'd

"Jesus saves! Esposito scores on the rebound."

patiently climbed the ladder, paying his dues and learning the system cold. In 1967, Schmidt replaced Emms as G.M. and the masterpiece began to take shape. Bucyk was the capstone. Johnston, Green, defensive artist Eddie Westfall, and a pair of rugged defensemen, Don Awrey and Dallas Smith, slowly developed during the bad years. In 1965, they stole Gerry Cheevers from Toronto. In 1966, they stole Johnny McKenzie from the Rangers, obtaining him for "Cement Head." From Detroit they got fearless Gary Doak, who had a "B" stitched to his chest. Schmidt's epic deal for Esposito, Hodge, and Stanfield followed in 1967, although Milt remains equally proud of getting madcap Eddie Shack from the Leafs the same day. "It was Eddie who lit the spark of that team," Schmidt contends. Brash Derek Sanderson, who fancied himself the poor man's Orr, came from the farm system, followed by Wayne Cashman, Glen "Slats" Sather, Ace Bailey, Don Marcotte, and the intellectual defenseman Rickie Smith. The "Big Bad Bruins" were in place. Immaturity cost them the Cup in 1969 when they let their ancient Montreal adversaries deny them. But in 1970, they blew everybody away.

You had to be there to appreciate the scope of "Bruins fever" in the Cup Years. Hockey rinks sprouted everywhere. They were seen by their adoring fans as sons of God, which, Scott Fitzgerald reminds us, means exactly what it says. When a star speeding in his fancy car clipped a pedestrian, editorialists lamented the arrogance of jaywalkers. People rode around with bumper stickers that read, "Jesus saves! Esposito scores on the rebound." Moms wanted their boys to grow up to be Bobby Orr; Dads wanted their daughters to marry him. When a rowdy player got jailed for tearing apart a bar, he used his one legal telephone call to order Chinese food. It was how a "Gashouse Gang" ought to behave and people loved it.

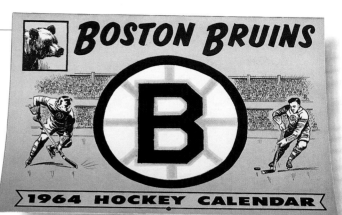

Their chippiness and swagger did not amuse traditionalists, who saw them as "bad winners." A Toronto columnist moaned that their pregame meal consisted of "ugly pills." A rival G.M. observed, "When they drop the puck to start the game, the Bruins think it's a piece of raw meat." The Rangers' Brad Park, who in a later incarnation became one of their best and brightest, called them "dirty, spoiled brats." All the controversy only inspired them more and they went on raising hell, on and off the ice. In a hotel brawl, one of the stars, enraged by a perceived insult to his wife, tossed a teammate through a plate-glass window. No hotel was safe.

They broke one up in Toronto and ran wild in a North Shore country club. They almost lost a defenseman one snowy night in Michigan when the lad, flushed with drink, fell out of a hotel window. But they hung together at all costs and that was admirable. "We got 18 players and each one will fight for the other 17," Sanderson once boasted to me. "And if someone gets taken out and can't get the bastard that did him in, then someone else will pick up the banner. Sooner or later, we'll get him."

As long as Sinden was coach, the zaniness was no problem. "I worked the crap out of them in practice," Harry says. "They knew their fun was over when the damn practice started. I made them pay big time every workout because I knew what kind of characters they were and how much fun they were having, and I didn't want them to think for one moment that the game on the ice was another rose garden. I never knew exactly what they were doing, but I wanted them to know that if they went too far with the nightlife, when practice started they were likely to die." It was a policy that worked well, but two days after winning the Cup, at the height of the civic carnival it inspired, Sinden quit when Weston Adams humiliated him over a lousy two grand in a contract hassle. It was the Adams clan's dumb-

Runaway expansion came to the NHL just as the Bruins farm system was ripening in a bumper crop of superb prospects like Bernie Parent, left, the brilliant goalie. Parent was one of seven ex-Bruins on the Flyer team that stole the Cup from Boston in 1974.

est stunt in the half century they owned the team. Tom Johnson followed. Product of the classy Canadiens tradition, he gave them a long leash, allowing the 1971 team to romp as no NHL team ever had. They had four 100-point scorers, seven of the top ten scorers, and ten 20-goal scorers. No team had ever won more games (57), scored more goals (399), tallied more points (1,093), or broken more records in a single season (40). Yet they lost to Montreal in the playoffs because they blew a 5–1 lead in the second game when hubris conned them into thinking they were so good they could even toy with "the Curse." A generation later, a still fuming Orr told Joe Fitzgerald, the HERALD'S estimable hockey writer: "You know what that was all about? That was called 'sitting on a lead' and when I think about it even now I get mad at myself and my teammates because you never, ever sit on a lead against a great team." Angered, they steamrolled in 1971–72 with Esposito (133 points) and Orr

Some called Phil Esposito, above, "the Roman" because he had bearing and a lordly confidence. When Milt Schmidt stole Esposito, Ken Hodge,

and Fred Stanfield from Chicago in 1967, it inevitably became known as "the greatest heist since the Brinks." It was a caper worthy of Al Capone,

and it took place but two hundred yards from the scene of the notorious 1950 robbery. Schmidt had more trouble convincing his own boss, the

very unpleasant Hap Emms, than the Blackhawks. Emms didn't mind trading tiny Pit Martin and goalie Jack Norris. But he loathed parting with his

pet, defenseman Gilles Marotte. "I finally called Tommy Ivan and said 'OK' even without Hap's approval," Schmidt recalls. "Hap didn't speak to me

for two weeks." But it hardly mattered. A month later Emms was also gone. Esposito, Hodge, and Stanfield scored 878 goals for the Bruins.

(117) again running amok. They regained the Cup as Orr, on one good leg, put on a show against the Rangers that still makes crusty hockey men weep when they recall it. But sitting in the stands, the exiled Sinden didn't like what he saw. "While they won it, I still thought they looked fat," he said recently. "Physically or in the head?" I asked. "Both," he replied. "They had lost their edge." And then they lost Green, Cheevers, McKenzie, Westfall, and Sanderson in the off-season raids of NHL expansion and the new free-spending World Hockey Association.

Sinden, fresh from Team Canada's historic joust with the Soviet Union, returned that fall as G.M. and had his fears confirmed. He deposed his pal Tom Johnson in favor of raspy Bep Guidolin, the wartime phenom, who as coach would promptly alienate everyone. While the Bruins fell to the Rangers in the 1973 Playoffs, Esposito's knee was wrecked by a Ron Harris check; the sort of insult they used to deliver, not take. The injury inspired another chapter in their legend when Espo's chums wheeled him out of the hospital and into a nearby saloon late at night so he could attend their season-ending frolic. It was a stunt orchestrated by the late and fabled John "Frosty" Forristall, assistant trainer and poet laureate of the Big Bads. Frosty's fingerprints were on all their best antics. But the party was almost over. In the '74 Finals the expansion Flyers shocked them in a dandy opus featuring Kate Smith's

"God Bless America" renditions, which whipped the Philadelphians into a frenzy. It ended with an angry Orr sitting in the penalty box, victim of a horrible call in a 1–0 game. On a facade above him, nutty Flyer fans had posted a banner reading: "Linda Lovelace says the Bruins will choke!" It was mortifying and it got uglier. Guidolin stormed away from the team, charging: "Esposito is the Godfather of that damn team and Sinden is too scared to do anything about it. I got tired of being shafted." The unknown Don Cherry, who'd spent his entire life in the bushes, took over. After one more troubled season Sinden pulled the plug on the era by trading Esposito and the very able Carol Vadnais for the Rangers' fallen angels Brad Park and Jean Ratelle. The lads were in Vancouver the night of the trade and marked the occasion by trashing a hotel room. Wayne Cashman got socked with a hefty bill for the damages, but he was not alone. The entire gang wept bitterly that night, for they knew it was over.

With poetic license, the late Herb Ralby dubbed Vic Stasiuk, Bronco Horvath, and John Bucyk "the Uke line." Bronco, the elusive centerman, lost the 1959–60 scoring title when he took sick in the final game, while Bobby Hull was scrounging two assists to beat him by one point.

DEPARTURE OF ORR

Bobby Orr's contract war with the Bruins that led to his shocking departure in the spring of 1976 had historic impact. We are accustomed to such carnivals today. Back then, they were new. It was one of the first mega-buck brawls involving the issue of a player's right to bolt. The controversy was huge and left permanent scars, with Harry Sinden and the Bruins being unfairly cast as the bad guys. You still hear media wiseguys spout about how "Harry traded Bobby Orr," which is nonsense. In his sanctified stature, Orr's motives are rarely questioned. But having been there I can tell you he did not cover himself with glory in this particular fight. When he was young, he was very stubborn.

But the real villain—as all the world knows, now that he's ended up in jail—was Orr's outsized, flamboyant, acerbic, self-aggrandizing, bully of a barrister, Alan "the Eagle" Eagleson, who was considered a cinch to eventually become Canada's prime minister before he got on the high road of big profits that led to the can. Orr was impressed by the politically important when he was young, and he was utterly devoted to the haughty Eagle. And it's absolutely true that their alliance was fabulously successful for years. Every contract Eagle landed for Bobby broke new ground, benefiting every other player.

It's a convoluted tale—it took 20 years for the Eagle's tracks to be traced. And he might still be strutting had it not been for the dogged, heroic reporting of Russ Conway of the Lawrence EAGLE-TRIBUNE, who should have won the Pulitzer Prize for which he was nominated. Thanks mainly to Conway, everyone knows at last what Eagleson was all about.

Sadly, Orr paid a terrific price in terms of money he had but didn't keep plus money he could have had but never got. People today claim to be surprised to learn Orr would be part-owner of the Bruins were it not for Eagle's antics. Yet that was never a secret. The day before he defected for Chicago, even as Eagle was branding the Bruins' offers "insulting," the GLOBE'S Fran Rosa wrote: "Orr has been offered 18.6 percent of the Bruins franchise with the option of selling it back at any time. We should all be insulted the same way." The Bruins' new owners, the Jacobs boys from Buffalo, were seen as sinister characters with bad reputations. So it was easy for Orr to tune them out, much as Eagle wished. I also reported that Orr was making a mistake and not getting all the facts. So did the HERALD'S Leo Monahan. But Orr listened to no one but Eagle. And when I challenged Eagle and his "alleged" facts at a Montreal news conference, he threatened to punch me in the nose. Actually, he used the word "tweak" not "punch." I'll say this for the Eagle: he had plenty of gall. After Eagelson went to jail in January 1998, Orr joined with 40 of his fellow immortals in a campaign, organized by Brad Park, to have the man he once called his "father figure" ingloriously booted out of the Hockey Hall of Fame.

But the hockey gods work in strange ways. The tender interlude that followed was even better—Don "Grapes" Cherry's "Lunchpail Gang," who had only four seasons (1975–79) in the sun. They were the perfect foil of the Canadiens, who broke their hearts three years running. No team ever worked harder, and no team was more of a pleasure to be associated with. Players don't change much, so maybe it was cosmic or chemistry. Certainly the coach, in his often wacky way, had a lot to do with it. "Grapes" had his flaws, Lord knows, and he kind of blew it in the end and had to be carried off on his shield, sputtering. But no coach of anything had a keener sense of sport as entertainment. He was hockey's "Music Man"—an engaging rascal, a pure romantic. His charm redeemed his antics, and his yearning for something magic after years as an outcast was touching. It was a great story, and a great team, although Grapes masterfully promoted the illusion that his lads were just humble overachievers. Balderdash! Cheevers, Ratelle, Park, O'Reilly, Bucyk, Cashman, Middleton, Marcotte, and McNab were Hall-of-Fame quality. They were backed up by a host of character actors worthy of a David Lean movie: Milbury, Schmautz, Sheppard, Wensink, Doak, Smith, Jonathan, Miller, Foster, Sims, Gilbert, Pettie. "We were the toughest team ever," Cherry insists. "You know what Dave 'the Hammer' Schultz said about us in his book? He said, 'We Flyers had five tough guys. The Bruins had five tough guys and five nuts guys. I couldn't sleep the night before a game at the Boston Garden.' How's that!" For Grapes, it's still glorious.

At 27, Gordie Kluzak, who had brilliant promise, had to quit in 1991 after 11 surgical procedures on his knees. Rather than sulk, he got into Harvard, graduated, then went on to Harvard Business School. It's a great sports story and maybe, given the nature of the times, unique.

At the height of his wheeler-dealer powers, Sinden pulled outrageous larcenies. He got Cheevers back in 1975 after three miserable seasons in the WHA. People said Cheesie was dead inside. One game back in the Garden restored him. From Buffalo in 1976 came Peter McNab, who provided huge offense. In 1976 Sinden fleeced the Rangers out of Rick Middleton for Ken Hodge, who'd twice been a 100-point scorer but was 10 years older. "Rickie was a turkey when he came to us," Cherry notes. "He looked like Porky Pig. But he became the all-time example of how good pulling on a Bruins jersey could be for a guy."

The key, though, was trading Esposito in the deal for Park and Ratelle. It took guts. Sinden was ridiculed for letting him go. The local dean of sports radio called him "a schmoo." New York "experts" sneered. Said nasty columnist Dick Young: "Goodbye Brad Park; au revoir, Jean Ratelle. Take with you all the Stanley Cups you won for us. You can wear them." But Sinden knew better, and when Orr crashed and fled in 1976, the trade saved the team. "I used to call Brad

> ## "On skates, Terry is about as smooth as a stucco bathtub."
>
> —Bobby Orr

'truck driver tough,'" Sinden says. "I told him one time, 'I don't think I ever got more pleasure watching a guy play than you.' Maybe I identified with him. No one could identify with Orr. He was God." Even more surprising were the Ratelle dividends. Leo Monahan's scouting report on "Ratty" is right on: "An exceptional player. A whiz defensively. Good on face-offs. Great playmaker and skater. Gives you an honest effort every night. Classy. Went to church all the time. Never swore. You couldn't find anything wrong with the guy. He was wonderful."

So was Terry O'Reilly, another important member of the Lunchpail Gang, in his different way. When he came up in 1973 his skating was horrible. One year Sanderson gave him a pair of double-runners for Christmas. "On skates, Terry is about as smooth as a stucco bathtub," Orr was quoted as saying. But as a noted adversary, Flyers coach Fred Shero, once observed, "Skating is overrated. O'Reilly always arrives at his destination on time—and with a bang!" Conventions did not apply to Terry. His focus was eerie; his pugnacity scary. Yet he was

one of the most thoughtful and principled men I've met in any walk of life. I concluded he came from a different place and time, maybe the Middle Ages. I could see him as a monastic scholar turned obsessed reformer. If I had to go to war and could take one man with me, it would be O'Reilly.

This, then, was the team Sinden put together and Cherry galvanized, and that was his great skill, the ability to unite and fire his forces. Alas, in the end, Grapes Himself became the biggest star and that drove a wedge between him and Harry. The best buddies became bitter foes. It was needless and a shame.

Three straight springs they had epic play-off showdowns with Montreal. Twice the road led

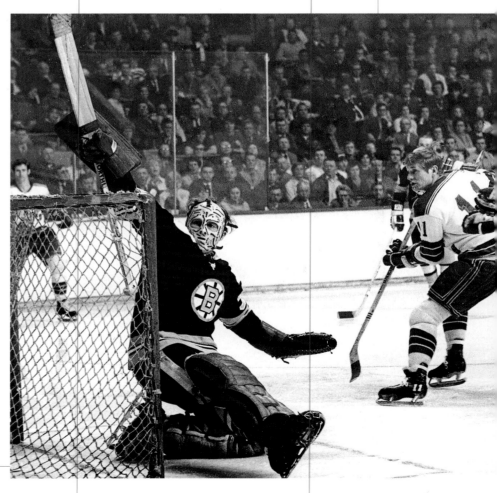

through Philadelphia, where they had the sort of rumbles usually found in alleys. In their sweep of the Flyers in 1977 they won back-to-back overtime ordeals at the Spectrum. It was in-your-face grinding at its most fierce. Cherry's teams were masters of hockey triage. After one of the thrillers, "Doctor Hook," Bob Schmautz, had to be carried off, having turned gray. Unbelievably, Brad Park was on the ice more than 60 minutes. They played games as hard as was humanly possible. They were also still crazy. In Los Angeles, the Kings unwisely tried the Flyers' trick and had a tenor warble "God Bless America" at the start. Cashman and Frosty Forristall cut the Forum's microphone cable. When the guy started to sing, there was silence. Regrettably, all roads led to Montreal, who swept them in 1977. The next year, they went down in flames in a series memorable for Cheevers's valor. Behind two games in the finals, the Bruins were greeted by a great Garden crowd who rose at the start of game three to give the round, balding goalie a three-minute ovation, chanting, "Cheevers . . . Cheevers . . . Cheevers." It was chilling, for the dark, old, gothic arena generated such sound and mood like no other place. Cheevers responded with a shutout. The next game, in an unforgettably brutal moment, Cherry's pit bull Stan Jonathan whaled Montreal's Pierre Bouchard, who was seven inches taller and 30 pounds

Gerry Cheevers, left, rebuffs Ranger Vic Hadfield. Blending a gambler's nonchalance with a furious competitive spirit, "Cheesie" was the all-time "team player." Equally a crowd-pleaser was Stanley Jonathan, below, seen pinning a foe twice his size. A full-blooded Tuscarora from Six Nations, Stan now runs a hockey school for Indian kids.

Following spread: Thrashing at the Capitals' goal mouth is Adam Oates, while Jozef Stumpel (16) and Rick Tocchet converge.

heavier, to within what seemed an inch of his life. Thus inspired, the Bruins won in overtime when the zany Schmautz took a Sheppard feed and drilled a low dart past Ken Dryden, producing as much ecstasy as I've ever seen anywhere for any purpose. "I can smell it and taste it," bellowed Park. But the Habs took the next two and the '78 Cup. They met again in the '79 Semifinals where the Bruins suffered their most infamous lapse. Hanging to a 4–3 lead with 74 seconds left, they had too many men on the ice. "Sometimes in the retelling it seems as if there were a brass band on the ice, every member wearing a Bruins uniform," wrote Leigh Montville. "Who loses a game, a series (a Cup?) because too many men are on the ice?"

DON CHERRY

He's a Canadian TV star now, as influential as Howard Cosell once was in the States. He's famed for his outlandish dress and booming presence. He's the "cock of the walk" and he knows it. He also knows he's come a long way from the days he struggled to provide for his beloved Rose and the kids, making

of conformists. He is a character. He is "Grapes," a keeper of the flame.

His NHL career consisted of exactly one playoff game with the Bruins in 1955, a 5–1 loss in Montreal. "My big claim to fame was that I knocked down Jean Beliveau and got my picture in the paper. It wasn't legal.

they ate them all." Only 21 and deemed a hot prospect, it should have been just the beginning. But in defiance of team orders, he played baseball that summer and broke his shoulder, profoundly alienating Bruins boss Lynn Patrick. "He thought I wasn't trying because I wanted to stay with Rose in Hershey, where we'd met the year before. But the truth was my shoulder was still bleeding from the operation. I'd wake up at training camp and there would be blood all over the pillow, and I went to Hammy Moore, the trainer, and told him the eight-inch cut in my shoulder was opening. You know what he did? He gave me 30 Band-Aids. Back in those days, if you did something they didn't like, you landed in 'the Bad Book.' That's where I ended up. And just to prove how much they disliked me, they sent me to the Darth Vader of Hockey, Eddie Shore. It was like being sent to Devil's Island."

If Shore's idiosyncrasies were fascinating as a player, they made him harsh and abusive as an owner. To the luckless kids indentured to his

Springfield Indians, he was a tyrant and a skinflint. "He was a very insensitive and mean man. He had no feelings for anybody. He would suspend guys who hadn't played in a month for 'indifferent play' just so he could get the payroll down. We had a goaltender named Georgie Woods who kept dropping down for shots and Shore said, 'Quit doing that.' So to stop him Shore tied a rope to the top of

the cross-bar around Georgie's neck. It was a short rope too. He was completely off his rocker." Shore called Cherry "the Madagascar Kid," the implication being that if he got out of line, that's where he'd be shipped. Yet, even while his life was being made miserable, Cherry could not help but be in awe of the old man. "Even at the age

peanuts playing bush league hockey in the winter and more peanuts doing heavy construction in the summer. Donald Stewart Cherry can be infuriating if you cross him. But he's a valuable commodity in an unsentimental world

I cross-checked him from behind. Oh well. My mother was there to watch me with my Aunt Tillie and they brought me cookies. All the players made fun of me coming on the train back to Boston with these cookies. But

Grapes's NHL career consisted of one 1955 playoff game with the Bruins.

of 60, he could take a two on one and somehow nail the guy with the puck. At 60 he could skate as fast backward as most of us could skate forward. He could actually skate with no laces in his skates. He was a marvel. But as a person and coach of young men, he was a disaster." Four years with Shore were but a slice of Cherry's 16 years pounding the bushes; "hockey's Siberia," he calls it. "Sure I was bitter."

It was Harry Sinden who plucked him from exile in 1974, handing him custody of Bobby Orr, Phil Esposito, and company after he'd coached well at Rochester. Cherry's gratitude was boundless. "The first four years of Harry and I were like a honeymoon. I could hardly wait to have a few beers with him after the game." Sinden's recollection is equally mellow. Sinden says, "We had so much fun. When the British and Scottish bands came to town, we'd go see them together and he'd say, 'You can't go without having a few beers because you don't cry over the music if you haven't had some beers.' Can't you just see us there with the pipes playing and the tears running down our faces?" All of which made their messy breakdown in 1979 the more sad. In his Boston years, Grapes increasingly strutted his eccentricities: dressing like the Duke of Windsor, promoting his beloved bull-terrier, Blue, as assiduously as the team, charming the media with bombastic dissertations on Lord Horatio Nelson and Sir Francis Drake. Grapes's rise to cult status gnawed on Harry, as did his policy of driving a wedge between the team and the front office, part of Grapes's "us against them" tactic. In the 1979 season the childish sniping between the two became fierce, leading to a crashing denouement in Montreal—the epic "too many men on the ice" conclusion in the playoff semifinals. Sinden still believes the Bruins should have won the Stanley Cup that year. The split came a few days later. Will McDonough and I forced them to try to settle their differences by arranging a secret meeting at a Chinese restaurant in the suburbs. It failed. Too much had been said. They were both hardheaded and full of a lot of Scottish blood, as well as music.

But some 20 years later, Cherry makes a remarkably frank concession. "I blame myself a lot for what happened that last year. I started to think I was God. You get so successful and your team is the toughest team in the toughest game in sports, and you start thinking it's all you. There's no doubt I turned the players against Harry . . . but then he made it easy for me to do it." Sinden also admits the rift still bothers him. "Yes, it does," Sinden says. "Because there was no reason for it to happen." The problem in the end was they were too much alike.

The beaming Cherry returns to the Garden in 1995.

The Bruins did! You could look it up. Whereupon the quixotic Cherry, outrageous to the last, walked away from the team. His ongoing feud with his old pal Sinden, a clash of huge egos, was beyond repair. He seemed, Will McDonough artfully observed, like Colonel Nickerson in THE BRIDGE OVER THE RIVER KWAI. He had taken his ragged but gallant band to the brink and then marched them, with full honors and braying bagpipes, straight into the abyss. Ah, but what fun it had been.

Though gone, Cherry cast a shadow over the '80s. Three of his pets—Cheevers, O'Reilly, and Milbury—each coached in succession with a distinction that still fell short of the ultimate prize. All three perpetuated "the Lunchpail style" with its emphasis on a stern work ethic, strident manliness, and a high tolerance for pain. But some began to wonder if it was the best policy in the modern game, and Milbury, flirting with heresy, edged toward a less grinding and more open, less physical and more breezy style, with mixed results. Genes are not casually altered.

Through the decade, they prevailed another hockey generation, doggedly making the playoffs year after year and even mildly challenging for the Cup itself, now and again. More fabulous Sinden larcenies made what success they had possible. A draft pick heisted from the Kings in exchange for a reserve goalie resulted in Ray Bourque, and then in June 1986, Sinden, in a caper that still must make him privately glow, sent Barry Pederson, a fine and courageous center who had won a battle with cancer, to Vancouver for a pick that resulted in defenseman Glen Wesley plus right winger Cam Neely. Other Sinden deals imported useful characters like Pete Peeters, Ken Linseman, Adam Oates, Charlie Simmer, Andy Moog, Bob Carpenter, Andy Brickley, and Mike O'Connell, now of the front office. Some nice prospects were developed: Bruce Crowder and his brother Keith, who was a kind of quiet Cashman; checking whiz Steve Kasper, who bedeviled Gretzky; Al Pedersen; Dave Reid; "Stumper" Burridge; the B.C.

The young Cam Neely wedges between the Habs' Rick Green and Patrick Roy. He was 25 when he sustained his ruinous hip injury and never again had a full season. His 50 goals in 49 games (1993–94) suggest what might have been.

Below: It mattered not to Gerry Cheevers whether he won 2–1 or 7–6. He was utterly indifferent to personal statistics. Good at many games, like his dad, he had the perfect sports temperament. Said writer Frank Orr, "Gerry Cheevers is a man who knows how to live."

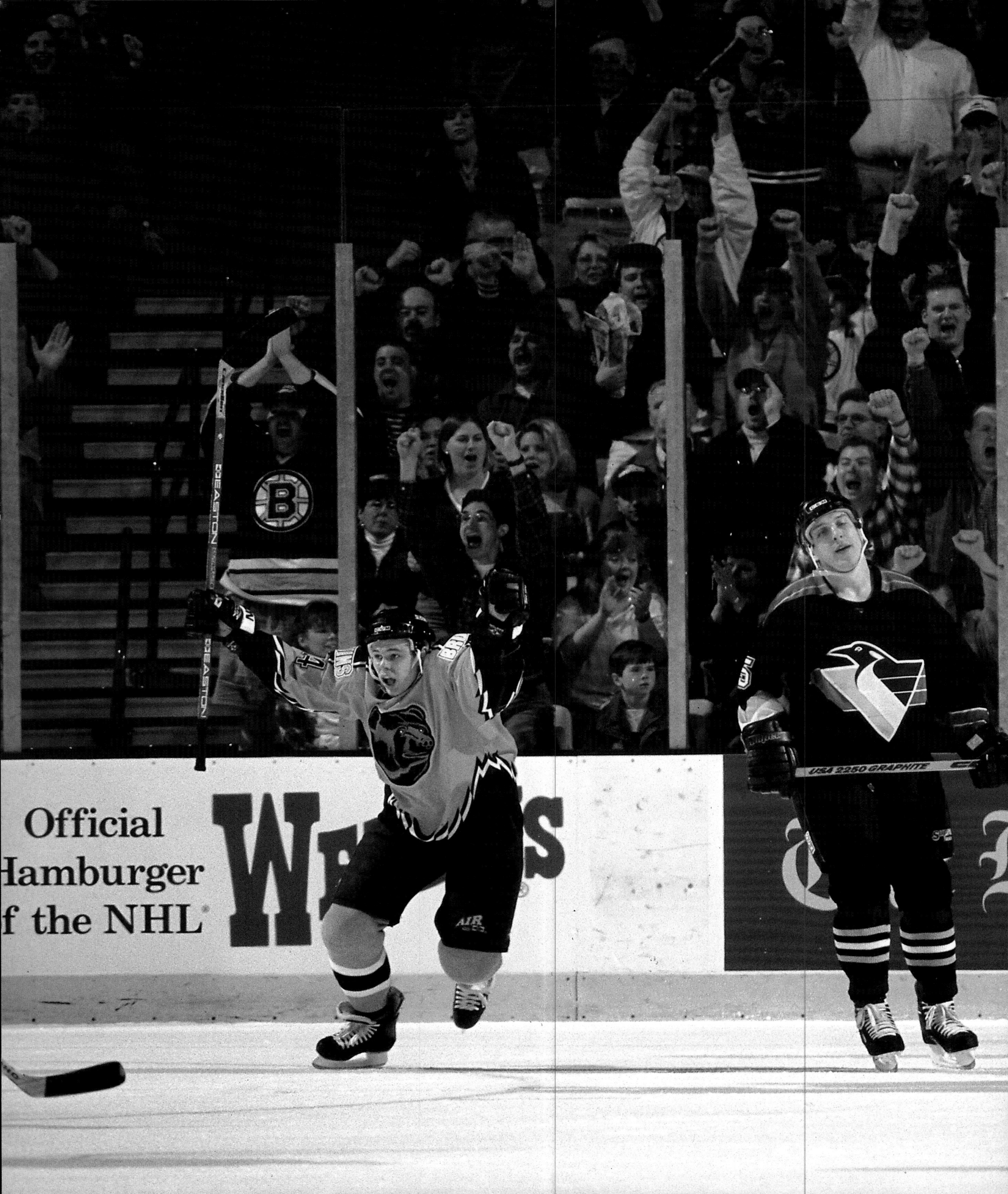

Official
Hamburger
of the NHL

The Bruins went 29 seasons (1968–96) without missing the playoffs, something no other team in pro sports can boast. But jaded veterans imported in the '90s greased a steady decline, and in 1996–97, they finished dead last. A painful rebuilding was predicted. But in 1997–98, they made one of the mightiest surges in sports history, charging back into the playoffs. Gritty Russians Sergei Samsonov and Dmitri Khristich, here scoring against the Penguins, were key factors while their linemate Jason Allison was taking the NHL by storm leading pundit Kevin Dupont to wonder if Allison could grow into a mini Phil Esposito. The resurgence of the 1997-98 season might have been even more dramatic save for a preposterous officiating call in the playoffs with Washington. Had not P. J. Axelsson's apparent, sudden-death goal in game three been nullified, the Bruins might have won the entire series. And then, who knows? Axelsson's goal was scratched because linemate Tim Taylor's toe had invaded the Capitals' crease, by about an inch. The seeming pettiness of the call enraged Harry Sinden as well as half the town but it may give Pat Burns' "kiddy corps" something to feed on. A lingering sense of injustice can galvanize a young team. "We deserved better, but I like what I see," said Ray Bourque when it was over. "The future looks pretty good for this team."

boys—Craig Janney and Steve Heinze, the Harvard boys—Don Sweeney and Ted Donato, and a pair of elegant rough-

necks, Jay Miller and Lyndon Byers. But with unexceptional drafting, and neither the means nor the will to spend big

money. Sinden's facile dealings were crucial and Bourque and Neely were his glory.

Consider the consequences had he not conned the Kings and Canucks.

On the other hand, you wonder what might have been had they not had so much

rotten luck. Had Orr been blessed with good knees, he might still be playing. Don't laugh.

Howe played longer. Defying conventional wisdom, Sinden chose a bright, lanky defenseman

with the wingspan of an eagle with the 1982 top pick, spurning the celebrated Brian Bellows.

Gordie Kluzak's knees proved to be weaker than Orr's, but in his two healthy seasons he

made it clear that with luck he would have been another Larry Robinson. Knee woes also

felled the arty Swede Michael Thelven. In 1982, they unveiled Mike Moffat, a refreshing boy-

next-door kind of kid in goal, and he was clearly a favorite of Cheevers the maestro. But Mike

couldn't take the strain, and after a gutty playoff effort against Quebec, he disappeared. Craig

MacTavish might have played twenty years for the Bruins but after he was involved in a

The critics roared when Jason

Allison, above, was obtained with

Anson Carter and Jim Carey at the

cost of aging, high-priced stars

Oates, Ranford, and Tocchet. A year

later, Allison was the star. Carter was

emerging. The critics were silent.

deadly alcohol-related car accident, Sinden gave him to distant Edmonton to help him get his life

back together. But the heartbreaker was the tragedy of Normand Leveille, a swift, smiling little

winger out of Chicoutimi whom the Bruins projected as another Yvan Cournoyer. At 19,

Norm had played only 75 games when a runaway blood clot left him semi-invalid for the

rest of his life. In that context, Cam Neely would insist his misfortune was piddling. Yet the

rare condition—called myositis ossificans—that eroded his thigh muscles surely slashed

at least six peak seasons from his career. It was also the biggest factor in the unraveling of

the Bruins in the '90s, since he was their essence. "He was the epitome of a hockey player" is the way Cherry

puts it. "If you ever needed to take a player to Mars to show the Martians what one looked like, the guy you'd take

would be Cam Neely."

All of that not withstanding, they had mighty moments in the contemporary era, with the Canadiens

remaining their supreme nemesis. A high note was sounded in 1983 when Park's overtime goal decided a rough

playoff series with the Sabres. The puck squirted loose from a melee in front and Park, pouncing catlike and whis-

pering to himself, "Stay down, stay flat," let go a 30-foot slapper that indeed stayed down and flat, and the place went

ballistic. The music of the Garden at such moments was always grand. But it ended in the next round against the

Islanders. In 1984, the last round of the ritual humiliations at the hands of Montreal began. Four more years they met the Habs and lost to the Habs, losing 13 of 15 and 8 straight in one stretch. Only once was it even close, in 1985, when Sinden was briefly back behind the bench, and they went to the last minute of the last game still scoreless. Then Mats Naslund, writhing like an eel, slid across the net and snapped a backhander home that nailed them. Once again. It was becoming absurd. "Hockey is unfair," said goalie Doug Keans. "Just like life." Aristotle could not have been more profound.

So it was that no highlight of the modern era surpasses the lifting of the jinx in 1988, when the Hard Hats finally beat the Top Hats amidst an aura of grudge and passion that the Hatfields and the McCoys could not have matched. The "thing" started as the Allies were chasing Rommel across North Africa and it ended while Bush and Dukakis were jousting for the presidency, and there was a whole lot of history in between. Boston's hero was Rejean Lemelin, native of Quebec, schooled in the myths of the Flying Frenchmen and a rarity for the Bruins, who had always—it was persistently whispered—shied away from French players, Ray Bourque aside, of course. Bourque was magnificent in that series, as were kids who later proved disappointing, Glen Wesley, Bob Joyce, and Craig Janney. But it was Lemelin in goal who did it. In the second game in Montreal, which they had to win because they'd lost the first, he stood on his head, flew through the air, stopped pucks with his face, and stashed the Habs like Horatio at the bridge, winning even the hosannas of the Forum savants. It was what had to happen; one guy standing up and saying, "Enough is enough!" They won the next three games handily and the Curse/Jinx/Hex, whatever, was finished. Most fittingly, they were coached by one who'd taken so many of the Canadiens' slings and arrows so very personally, Terence Joseph James O'Reilly, Himself.

It was a vintage year. In the next round, they beat New Jersey in a rumble memorable for its colorful uproar over the officiating. When Devils' coach, Jim Schoenfeld (an ex-Bruin, naturally) accosted portly referee Don Koharski and screamed, "Have another doughnut, you fat pig!" the officials' union demanded Schoenfeld's scalp. When they didn't get it, they went on strike requiring the Stanley Cup match to be officiated by scabs recruited from bush leagues. SPORTS ILLUSTRATED termed the scene "The theater of the absurd." And the Bruins moved on to the finals, where they were outclassed by Edmonton as Sir Wayne Gretzky put on a

Bobby Francis (left), son of "the Cat," Pat Burns (middle), the ex-Montreal cop, and Jacques Laperriere (right), a Norris Trophy winner with the Canadiens, lead the Bruins on-ice as they approach the millennium. The era ends much as it began, with an iron-willed Montreal native as coach. Like Art Ross, Pat Burns does not suffer hockey foolishness gladly.

clinic. They probably would have been swept had not the lights gone out late in game four, a power outage that Steve Nazro will want me to emphasize was in no way the fault of the too-much-abused Boston Garden, may she rest in peace. It

Joe Thornton, teen hopeful, Anson Carter, Steve Heinze and Mike Sullivan (up front) with young giant Hal Gill (looming in back), are among the identifiable "new age" Bruins savoring a goal. The 1998 team surprised everyone, except maybe the team of Burns, Sinden, and O'Connell. The revival was a coup for Pat Burns, long esteemed as a great teaching coach, and it strengthened Mike O'Connell's stature as Harry Sinden's heir apparent. But it was Sinden, edging into elder statesman status, who got the biggest boot out of it. "Hockey," Sinden has said, "is the simplest of games. There are no blackboard strategies, no subtle designs. You need only the courage to stand up, the stamina to skate, and the ability to work hard."

was really a rather sweet coda. The memory of those Bruins fans, so long put down by local wiseguys, marching out of that dark building with so much decorum remains special. The Bruins won something more than a Cup that year. They got the Canadiens off their back. In the '90s, they made sure the Curse was not only dispelled but buried by beating the Canadiens four times. If history has truly reversed itself, Montreal will next beat them in the playoffs of 2033.

By then both teams will have rebounded from their checkered ordeals of the '90s. In the booming global game that's fast emerging, that's not as easy to do as it once was. The Bruins got caught in a rough transition at a complex time. The erosion was sharp during the regimes of Brian Sutter and Steve Kasper. Many believe they bottomed out the night in January 1996 in Toronto that Kasper, frustrated by the team's drift, benched Kevin Stevens, who deserved it, and Cam Neely, who did not. The next season, they missed the playoffs for the first time since Lyndon Johnson was president.

In the spring of 1997, they proclaimed a new order by naming Pat Burns, the imposing ex-cop with the stern visage, as coach. He remains famed for his service to the Canadiens, of course, but Pat Burns is too independent to be chained to any one tradition. The rebuilding begins with teen phenoms; Joe Thornton and Sergei Samsonov; a rugged, young defenseman, Kyle McLaren, whom Ray Bourque likes to introduce as "the next Ray Bourque;" tireless Swede Per-Johan Axelsson; Concord giant Hal Gill; the Washington gents Jason Allison and Anson Carter; and a goalie Sinden says reminds him "just a little of Cheevers," Byron Dafoe. It's either heresy or marvelous news. The Harvard vets, Donato and Sweeney, along with the eternal Bourque and a new ruffian, Ken Baumgartner, remain around to keep the kids in line. This is the nucleus of the new order, with more kids on the way. We will see. So will Pat Burns!

THE STAT BOX

BRUINS STATISTICS

BRUINS STANLEY CUP TEAMS

1928-29: Cecil "Tiny" Thompson, Eddie Shore, Lionel Hitchman, Perk Galbraith, Eric Pettinger*, Frank Frederickson*, Mickey Mackay**, Red Green, Norman "Dutch" Gainor, Harry Oliver, Eddie Rodden, Aubrey "Dit" Clapper, Ralph "Cooney" Weiland, Lloyd Klein, Cy Denneny, Bill Carson, George Owen, Myles Lane, Coach Art Ross

1938-39: Bobby Bauer, Mel Hill, Bill "Flash" Hollett, Roy Conacher, Gord Pettinger, Milt Schmidt, Woody Dumart, Jack Crawford, Ray Getliffe, Frank Brimsek, Eddie Shore, Aubrey "Dit" Clapper, Bill Cowley, Jack Portlandt, Red Hamill, Ralph "Cooney" Weiland, Charlie Sands, Jack Shewchuk, Cecil "Tiny" Thompson, Coach Art Ross

1940-41: Bill Cowley, Des Smith, Aubrey "Dit" Clapper, Frank Brimsek, Bill "Flash" Hollett, John Crawford, Bobby Bauer, Pat McCreavy, Herb Cain, Mel Hill, Milt Schmidt, Woody Dumart, Roy Conacher, Terry Reardon, Art Jackson, Eddie Wiseman, Gordie Bruce, Robert Hamill, Jack Shewchuk, Coach Ralph "Cooney" Weiland

1969-70: Gerry Cheevers, Ed Johnston, Bobby Orr, Rick Smith, Dallas Smith, Bill Speer, Gary Doak, Don Awrey, Phil Esposito, Ken Hodge, John Bucyk, Wayne Carleton**, Wayne Cashman, Derek Sanderson, Fred Stanfield, Ed Westfall, John McKenzie, Jim Lorentz, Don Marcotte, Bill Lesuk, Dan Schock, Garnet "Ace" Bailey, Nick Beverley, Jim Harrison*, Ron Murphy, Frank Spring, Tom Webster, Barry Wilkins, Coach Harry Sinden

1971-72: Gerry Cheevers, Ed Johnston, Bobby Orr, Ted Green, Carol Vadnais**, Dallas Smith, Don Awrey, Phil Espoito, Ken Hodge, John Bucyk, Mike Walton, Wayne Cashman, Garnet "Ace" Bailey, Derek Sanderson, Fred Stanfield, Ed Westfall, John McKenzie, Don Marcotte, Garry Peters, Chris Hayes, Rick Smith*, Nick Beverley, Ivan Boldirev*,Ron Jones, Reg Leach*, Matt Ravlich, Doug Roberts, Terry O'Reilly, Bob Stewart*, Coach Tom Johnson

* Traded during season   ** Purchased during season

BRUINS PRESIDENTS

Charles F. Adams	Nov. 1, 1924 to 1936
Weston W. Adams, Sr.	1936 to 1951
Walter A. Brown	1951 to Sept. 1964
Weston W. Adams, Sr.	Sept. 1964 to Mar. 30, 1969
Weston W. Adams, Jr.	Mar. 31, 1969 to Sept. 30, 1975
Paul A. Mooney	Oct. 1, 1975 to Mar. 24, 1987
William D. Hassett, Jr.	Mar. 24, 1987 to Dec. 1, 1988
Harry Sinden	Dec. 1, 1988 to present

BRUINS GENERAL MANAGERS

Arthur Ross	Nov. 1, 1924 to 1953-54
Lynn Patrick	1953-54 to 1964-65
Leighton "Hap" Emms	1965-66 to 1966-67
Milt Schmidt	1967-68 to 1971-72
Harry Sinden	Oct. 5, 1972 to present

BRUINS COACHES

Arthur Ross	10924-25 to 1927-28
Cy Denneny	1928-29
Arthur Ross	1929-30 to 1933-34
Frank Patrick	1934-35 to 1935-36
Arthur Ross	1936-37 to 1938-39
Ralph "Cooney" Weiland	1939-40 to 1940-41
Arthur Ross	1941-42 to 1944-45
Aubrey "Dit" Clapper	1945-46 to 1948-49
George Boucher	1949-50
Lynn Patrick	1950-51 to Dec. 25, 1954
Milt Schmidt	Dec. 25, 1954 to 1960-61
Phil Watson	1961-62 to 1962-63
Milt Schmidt	1962-63 to 1965-66
Harry Sinden	1966-67 to 1969-70
Tom Johnson	1970-71 to Feb. 5, 1973
Bep Guidolin	Feb. 5, 1973 to 1973-74
Don Cherry	1974-75 to 1978-78
Fred Creighton	July 5, 1979 to Mar. 22, 1980
Harry Sinden	Mar. 22, 1980 to Apr. 22, 1980
Gerry Cheevers	July 7, 1980 to Feb. 13, 1985
Harry Sinden	Feb. 13, 1985 to Apr. 16, 1985
Butch Goring	May 6, 1985 to Nov. 5, 1986
Terry O'Reilly	Nov. 5, 1986 to May 1, 1989
Mike Milbury	May 16, 1989 to May 30, 1991
Rick Bowness	June 4, 1991 to June 8, 1992
Brian Sutter	June 9, 1992 to May 17, 1995
Steve Kasper	May 25, 1995 to April 18, 1997
Pat Burns	May 21, 1997 to present

BRUINS CAPTAINS

Lionel Hitchman	1927-28 to 1930-31
George Owen	1931-32
Aubrey "Dit" Clapper	1932-33 to 1937-38
Ralph "Cooney" Weiland	1938-39
Aubrey "Dit" Clapper	1939-40 to 1946-47
Jack Crawford	1946-47 to 1949-50
Milt Schmidt	1950-51 to 1953-54
Ed Sandford	1954-55
Ferny Flaman	1955-56 to 1960-61
Don McKenney	1961-62 to 1962-63
Leo Boivin	1963-64 to 1965-66
John Bucyk	1966-67; 1973-74 to 1976-77
Wayne Cashman	1977-78 to 1982-83
Terry O'Reilly	1983-84 to 1984-85
Rick Middleton & Ray Bourque	1985-86 to 1987-88
Ray Bourque	1988-89 to present

BRUINS LIFETIME LEADERS—1924-25 to 1997-98

Seasons		Games		Goals		Assists		Points	
Bucyk	21	Bucyk	1436	Bucyk	545	Bourque	1036	Bourque	1411
Clapper	20	Bourque	1372	Esposito	459	Bucyk	794	Bucyk	1339
Bourque	19	Cashman	1027	Middleton	402	Orr	624	Esposito	1012
Cashman	16	O'Reilly	891	Bourque	375	Esposito	553	Middleton	898
M. Schmidt	16	Middleton	881	Neely	344	Cashman	516	Orr	888
Dumart	15	Marcotte	868	Hodge	289	Middleton	496	Cashman	793
Shore	14	Dallas Smith	861	Cashman	277	O'Reilly	402	Hodge	674
Doak	13	Clapper	830	Orr	264	Hodge	385	O'Reilly	606
Marcotte	13	M. Schmidt	776	McNab	263	Oates	357	Neely	590
O'Reilly	13	Dumart	771	Marcotte	230	Cowley	346	McNab	587
Dallas Smith	12	Milbury	754	M. Schmidt	229	M. Schmidt	346	M. Schmidt	575
Flaman	12	Westfall	727	Clapper	228	McNab	324	Cowley	536
Middleton	12	Boivin	717	K. Crowder	219	Park	317	Oates	499

Penalty Minutes		Shutouts		Playoff Scoring	GP	G	A	PTS
O'Reilly	2095	Thompson	74	Bourque	162	34	112	146
Milbury	1552	Brimsek	35	Esposito	71	46	56	102
K. Crowder	1261	Johnston	27	Middleton	111	45	55	100
Cashman	1041	Cheevers	26	Bucyk	109	40	60	100
Shore	1038	Henry	24	Orr	74	26	66	92
Bourque	1033	Winkler	19	Cashman	145	31	57	88
Green	1029	Gilbert	16	Neely	86	55	32	87
Flaman	1002	Simmons	15	Hodge	86	34	47	81
Byers	959	Moog	13	Park	91	23	55	78
Dallas Smith	934	Sawchuk	11	McNab	79	38	37	75
Orr	924	Stewart	10	Janney	69	17	56	73
Neely	921	Peeters	9	O'Reilly	108	25	42	67
Miller	856	Gelineau	7	Marcotte	132	34	27	61

BRUINS ALL-TIME TOP 20 SCORERS

No	Player	Regular Season					Playoffs				
		GP	G	A	PTS	PIM	GP	G	A	PTS	PIM
1	Ray Bourque	1372	375	1036	1411	1033	162	34	112	146	135
2	John Bucyk	1436	545	794	1339	436	109	40	60	100	34
3	Phil Esposito	625	459	553	1012	512	71	46	56	102	86
4	Rick Middleton	881	402	496	898	124	111	45	55	100	17
5	Bobby Orr	631	264	624	888	924	74	26	66	92	107
6	Wayne Cashman	1027	277	516	793	1041	145	31	57	88	250
7	Ken R. Hodge	652	289	385	674	620	86	34	47	81	108
8	Terry O'Reilly	891	204	402	606	2095	108	25	42	67	335
9	Cam Neely	524	344	246	590	921	86	55	32	87	160
10	Peter McNab	595	263	324	587	111	79	38	37	75	16
11	Milt Schmidt	776	229	346	575	466	86	24	25	49	60
12	Bill Cowley	469	190	346	536	112	62	12	34	46	22
13	Adam Oates	368	142	357	499	123	42	11	37	48	20
14	Don Marcotte	868	230	255	485	317	132	34	27	61	81
15	Keith Crowder	607	219	258	477	1261	78	13	22	35	209
16	Dit Clapper	830	228	246	474	252	81	13	17	30	46
17	Don McKenney	592	195	267	462	189	34	13	20	33	8
18	Jean Ratelle	419	155	295	450	84	58	23	33	56	10
19	Woody Dumart	771	211	218	429	99	82	12	15	27	23
20	Barry Pederson	379	166	251	417	248	34	22	30	52	25

BRUINS ALL STARS

The following Bruins have been named to the NHL All-Star teams by the Professional Hockey Writers Association since its inception in 1930-31.

GOALTENDERS
FIRST TEAM

Frank Brimsek	(2)	39-42
Cecil "Tiny" Thompson	(2)	36-38
Pete Peeters	(1)	83

SECOND TEAM

Frank Brimsek	(6)	40-41-43-46-47-48
Cecil "Tiny" Thompson	(2)	31-35
Jim Henry	(1)	52

DEFENSEMEN
FIRST TEAM

Ray Bourque	(12)	80-82-84-85-87-88-90-91-92-93-94-96
Bobby Orr	(8)	68-69-70-71-72-73-74-75
Eddie Shore	(7)	31-32-33-35-36-38-39
Aubrey "Dit" Clapper	(3)	39-40-41
Brad Park	(2)	76-78
Bill Quackenbush	(1)	51
Jack Crawford	(1)	46
Albert "Babe" Siebert	(1)	36

SECOND TEAM

Ray Bourque	(5)	81-83-86-89-95
Ferny Flaman	(3)	55-57-58
Aubrey "Dit" Clapper	(3)	31-35-44
Bill Quackenbush	(1)	53
Ted Green	(1)	69
Bobby Orr	(1)	67
Jack Crawford	(1)	43
Bill Hollett	(1)	43
Eddie Shore	(1)	34

CENTERS
FIRST TEAM

Phil Esposito	(6)	69-70-71-72-73-74
Bill Cowley	(4)	38-41-43-44
Milt Schmidt	(3)	40-47-51
Fleming Mackell	(1)	53

SECOND TEAM

Phil Esposito	(2)	68-75
Bronco Horvath	(1)	60
Milt Schmidt	(1)	52
Bill Cowley	(1)	45

LEFT WINGS
FIRST TEAM

John Bucyk	(1)	71

SECOND TEAM

Woody Dumart	(3)	40-41-47
Wayne Cashman	(1)	74
John Bucyk	(1)	68
Real Chevrefils	(1)	57
Ed Sandford	(1)	54
Herb Cain	(1)	44

RIGHT WINGS
FIRST TEAM

Ken R. Hodge	(2)	71-74

SECOND TEAM

Bobby Bauer	(4)	39-40-41-47
Cam Neely	(4)	88-90-91-94
Rick Middleton	(1)	82
John McKenzie	(1)	70

COACHES
FIRST TEAM

Ralph "Cooney" Weiland	(1)	41
Art Ross	(2)	38-43

SECOND TEAM

Art Ross	(1)	39

BRUINS IN THE HALL OF FAME

Charles F. Adams
Elected: 1960
Bruins: 1924-1936

Bobby Bauer
Elected: 1996
Bruins: 1935-42; 1945-47; 1951-52

Walter A. Brown
Elected: 1962
Bruins: 1951-1964

Gerry Cheevers
Elected: 1985
Bruins: 1965-72; 1975-80

Bill Cowley
Elected: 1968
Bruins: 1935-1947

Phil Esposito
Elected: 1984
Bruins: 1967-1976

Harvey Jackson
Elected: 1971
Bruins: 1941-1944

Harry Lumley
Elected: 1980
Bruins: 1957-1960

Harry Oliver
Elected: 1967
Bruins: 1926-1934

Brad Park
Elected: 1988
Bruins: 1975-1983

Bill Quackenbush
Elected: 1976
Bruins: 1949-1956

Terry Sawchuk
Elected: 1971
Bruins: 1955-1957

Albert "Babe" Siebert
Elected: 1964
Bruins: 1933-1936

Allan Stanley
Elected: 1981
Bruins: 1956-1958

Ralph "Cooney" Weiland
Elected: 1971
Bruins: 1928-1939

Weston W. Adams
Elected: 1972
Bruins: 1936-51; 1964-69

Leo Boivin
Elected: 1986
Bruins: 1954-1966

John Bucyk
Elected: 1981
Bruins: 1957-1978

Aubrey "Dit" Clapper
Elected: 1947
Bruins: 1927-1947

Cy Denneny
Elected: 1959
Bruins: 1928-29

Ferny Flaman
Elected: 1990
Bruins: 1945-52; 1954-56

Tom Johnson
Elected: 1970
Bruins: 1963-1965

Mickey MacKay
Elected: 1952
Bruins: 1928-1930

Bobby Orr
Elected: 1979
Bruins: 1966-1976

Jacques Plante
Elected: 1978
Bruins: 1972-73

Jean Ratelle
Elected: 1985
Bruins: 1975-1981

Milt Schmidt
Elected: 1961
Bruins: 1936-42; 1946-55

Harry Sinden
Elected: 1983
Bruins: 1966-Present

Nels Stewart
Elected: 1962
Bruins: 1932-35; 1936-37

Marty Barry
Elected: 1965
Bruins: 1929-1935

Frank Brimsek
Elected: 1966
Bruins: 1938-1949

Billy Burch
Elected: 1974
Bruins: 1932-1933

Sprague Cleghorn
Elected: 1958
Bruins: 1925-1928

Woody Dumart
Elected: 1992
Bruins: 1935-42; 1945-54

Frank Frederickson
Elected: 1958
Bruins: 1926-1929

Guy Lapointe
Elected: 1993
Bruins: 1983-84

Sylvio Mantha
Elected: 1960
Bruins: 1936-37

Bernie Parent
Elected: 1984
Bruins: 1965-1967

Walter "Babe" Pratt
Elected: 1966
Bruins: 1946-47

Arthur H. Ross
Elected: 1945
Bruins: 1924-1954

Eddie Shore
Elected: 1945
Bruins: 1926-1940

Reginald "Hooley" Smith
Elected: 1972
Bruins: 1936-37

Cecil "Tiny" Thompson
Elected: 1959
Bruins: 1928-1939

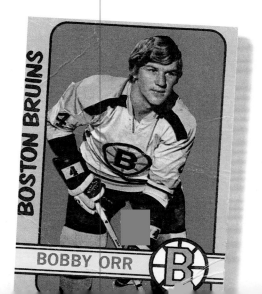

BOBBY ORR

BOSTON BRUINS TROPHY WINNERS

HART MEMORIAL TROPHY

Eddie Shore	1932-33
Eddie Shore	1934-35
Eddie Shore	1935-36
Eddie Shore	1937-38
Bill Cowley	1940-41
Bill Cowley	1942-43
Milt Schmidt	1950-51
Phil Esposito	1968-69
Bobby Orr	1969-70
Bobby Orr	1970-71
Bobby Orr	1971-72
Phil Esposito	1973-74

ART ROSS TROPHY

Ralph Weiland	1929-30
Milt Schmidt	1939-40
Bill Cowley	1940-41
Herb Cain	1943-44
Phil Esposito	1968-69
Bobby Orr	1969-70
Phil Esposito	1970-71
Phil Esposito	1971-72
Phil Esposito	1972-73
Phil Esposito	1973-74
Bobby Orr	1974-75

JAMES NORRIS MEMORIAL TROPHY

Bobby Orr	1967-68
Bobby Orr	1968-69
Bobby Orr	1969-70
Bobby Orr	1970-71
Bobby Orr	1971-72
Bobby Orr	1972-73
Bobby Orr	1973-74
Bobby Orr	1974-75
Bobby Orr	1974-75
Ray Bourque	1986-87
Ray Bourque	1987-88
Ray Bourque	1989-90
Ray Bourque	1990-91
Ray Bourque	1993-94

CALDER MEMORIAL TROPHY

Frank Brimsek	1938-39
Jack Gelineau	1949-50
Larry Regan	1956-57
Bobby Orr	1966-67
Derek Sanderson	1967-68
Ray Bourque	1979-80

VEZINA TROPHY

Cecil Thompson	1929-30
Cecil Thompson	1932-33
Cecil Thompson	1935-36
Cecil Thompson	1937-38
Frank Brimsek	1938-39
Frank Brimsek	1941-42
Pete Peeters	1982-83

LADY BYNG MEMORIAL TROPHY

Bobby Bauer	1939-40
Bobby Bauer	1940-41
Bobby Bauer	1946-47
Don McKenney	1959-60
John Bucyk	1970-71
John Bucyk	1973-74
Jean Ratelle	1975-76
Rick Middleton	1981-82

FRANK J. SELKE TROPHY

Steve Kasper	1981-82

CONN SMYTHE TROPHY

Bobby Orr	1969-70
Bobby Orr	1971-72

WILLIAM M. JENNINGS TROPHY

Reggie Lemelin & Andy Moog	1989-90

JACK ADAMS TROPHY

Don Cherry	1975-76

BILL MASTERTON MEMORIAL TROPHY

Charlie Simmer	1985-86
Gord Kluzak	1989-90
Cam Neely	1993-94

LESTER PATRICK TROPHY

Charles Adams	1967
Walter Brown	1968
Eddie Shore	1970
Ralph Weiland	1972
Weston Adams Sr.	1974
John Bucyk	1977
Tom Fitzgerald	1978
Art Ross	1984
Fred Cusick	1988
Milt Schmidt	1996

ELIZABETH C. DUFRESNE TROPHY

Cecil "Tiny" Thompson	1935-36
Eddie Shore	1936-37
Eddie Shore	1937-38
Eddie Shore	1938-39
Aubrey "Dit" Clapper	1939-40
Aubrey "Dit" Clapper	1940-41
Milt Schmidt	1941-42
Woody Dumart	1941-42
Bobby Bauer	1941-42
Frank Brimsek	1942-43
Bill Cowley	1943-44
Jack Crawford	1944-45
Jack Crawford	1945-46
Milt Schmidt	1946-47
Frank Brimsek	1947-48
Pat Egan	1948-49
Milt Schmidt	1949-50
Milt Schmidt	1950-51
Jim Henry	1951-52
Fleming Mackell	1952-53
Jim Henry	1953-54
Leo LaBine	1954-55
Terry Sawchuk	1955-56
Jerry Toppazzini	1956-57
Jerry Toppazzini	1957-58
Vic Stasiuk	1958-59
Bronco Horvath	1959-60
Leo Boivin	1960-61
Doug Mohns	1961-62
John Bucyk	1962-63
Ed Johnston	1963-64
Ted Green	1964-65
John Bucyk	1965-66
Bobby Orr	1966-67
Phil Esposito	1967-68
Phil Esposito	1968-69
Bobby Orr	1969-70
Phil Esposito	1970-71
Bobby Orr	1971-72
Phil Esposito	1972-73
Phil Esposito	1973-74
Bobby Orr	1973-74
Bobby Orr	1974-75
Gregg Sheppard	1975-76
Jean Ratelle	1976-77
Terry O'Reilly	1977-78
Brad Park	1977-78
Rick Middleton	1978-79
Ray Bourque	1979-80
Rick Middleton	1980-81
Rick Middleton	1981-82
Pete Peeters	1982-83
Rick Middleton	1983-84
Ray Bourque	1984-85
Ray Bourque	1985-86
Ray Bourque	1986-87
Cam Neely	1987-88
Randy Burridge	1988-89
Ray Bourque	1989-90
Cam Neely	1990-91
Vladimir Ruzicka	1991-92
Adam Oates	1992-93
Ray Bourque	1993-94
Cam Neely	1994-95
Ray Bourque	1995-96
Jozef Stumpel	1996-97
Jason Allison	1997-98

BOSTON BRUINS ALL-TIME ROSTER

A

ABBOTT, George	1943–44
ADAMS, John	1972–73
ADDUONO, Rick	1975–76
ALDCORN, Gary	1960–61
ALLISON, Jason	1996–97 - 1997–98
ANDERSON, Bill	1942–43
ANDERSON, Earl	1974–75 - 1976–77
ARBOUR, John	1965–66; 1967–68
ARMSTRONG, Bob	1950–51 - 1961–62
ARNIEL, Scott	1991–92
ASHBEE, Barry	1965–66
ASHTON, Brent	1991–92 - 1992–93
ATKINSON, Steve	1968–69
AUBUCHON, Oscar	1942–43 - 1943–44
AWREY, Don	1963–64 - 1972–73
AXELSSON, P. J.	1997–98

B

BABANDO, Pete	1947–48 - 1948–49
BAILEY, Garnet "Ace"	1968–69 - 1972–73
BAILEY, Scott	1995–96 - 1996–97
BALES, Mike	1992–93
BALFOUR, Murray	1964–65
BALUIK, Stan	1959–60
BANKS, Darren	1992–93 - 1993–94
BARAHONA, Ralph	1990–91 - 1991–92
BARON, Marco	1979–80 - 1982–83
BARR, Dave	1981–82 - 1982–83
BARRY, Eddie	1946–47
BARRY, Marty	1929–30 - 1934–35
BARRY, Ray	1951–52
BARTLETT, Jimmy	1960–61
BATES, Shawn	1997–98
BAUER, Bobby	1935–36 - 1941–42; 1945–46 - 1946–47; 1951–52
BAUMGARTNER, Ken	1997–98/
BEATTIE, Red	1930–31 - 1937–38
BECKETT, Bob	1956–57 - 1957–58; 1961–62; 1963–64
BEDDOES, Clayton	1995–96 - 1996–97
BEERS, Bob	1989–90 - 1991–92; 1996–97
BELANGER, Yves	1979–80
BENNETT, Bill	1978–79
BENNETT, Harvey	1944–45
BENSON, Bobby	1924–25
BERALDO, Paul	1987–88 - 1988–89
BERGDINON, Fred	1925–26
BERTHIAUME, Daniel	1991–92
BESSLER, Phil	1935–36
BETTIO, Sam	1949–50
BEVERLEY, Nick	1966–67; 1969–70; 1971–72 - 1973–74
BIBEAULT, Paul	1944–45 - 1945–46
BILLINGTON, Craig	1994–95 - 1995–96
BIONDA, Jack	1956–57 - 1958–59
BITTNER, Dick	1949–50
BLACKBURN, Don	1962–63
BLAKE, Mickey	1935–36
BLUE, John	1992–93 - 1993–94
BLUM, John	1983–84 - 1985–86; 1987–88; 1989–90
BODNAR, Gus	1953–54 - 1954–55
BOIVIN, Leo	1954–55 - 1965–66
BOLDIREV, Ivan	1970–71 - 1971–72
BOLL, Frank	1942–43 - 1943–44
BONIN, Marcel	1955–56
BOONE, Carl	1956–57 - 1957–58
BOUCHER, Billy	1926–27
BOURQUE, Ray	1979–80 - 1997–98
BOUTILIER, Paul	1986–87

BOYD, Irwin	1931–32; 1942–43 - 1943–44
BRACKENBOROUGH, John	1925–26
BRADLEY, Bart	1949–50
BRENNAN, Tom	1943–44 - 1944–45
BRICKLEY, Andy	1988–89 - 1991–92
BRIMSEK, Frank	1938–39 - 1942–43; 1946–47 - 1948–49
BRODERICK, Ken	1973–74 - 1974–75
BROOKS, Ross	1972–73 - 1974–75
BROWN, Adam	1951–52
BROWN, Wayne	1953–54
BRUCE, Gordie	1940–41 - 1941–42; 1945–46
BUCHANAN, Ron	1966–67
BUCYK, John	1957–58 - 1977–78
BURCH, Billy	1932–33
BUREGA, Bill	1955–56
BURKE, Eddie	1931–32
BURNS, Charlie	1959–60 - 1962–63
BURRIDGE, Randy	1985–86 - 1990–91
BYCE, John	1989–90 - 1991–92
BYERS, Gordon	1949–50
BYERS, Lyndon	1983–84 - 1991–92

C

CAFFERY, Jack	1956–57 - 1957–58
CAHILL, Charles	1925–26 - 1926–27
CAIN, Herb	1939–40 - 1945–46
CALLADINE, Norm	1942–43 - 1944–45
CAMPBELL, Wade	1985–86 - 1987–88
CAPUANO, Jack	1991–92
CAREY, Jim	1996–97 - 1997–98
CARLETON, Wayne	1969–70 - 1970–71
CARPENTER, Bob	1988–89 - 1991–92
CARROLL, George	1925–26
CARSON, Bill	1928–29 - 1929–30
CARTER, Anson	1996–97 - 1997–98
CARTER, Billy	1960–61
CARTER, John	1985–86 - 1990–91
CARVETH, Joe	1946–47 - 1947–48
CASEY, Jon	1993–94
CASHMAN, Wayne	1964–65; 1967–68 - 1982–83
CHADWICK, Ed	1961–62
CHAMBERLAIN, Murph	1942–43
CHAPMAN, Art	1930–31 - 1933–34
CHEEVERS, Gerry	1965–66 - 1971–72; 1975–76 - 1979–80
CHERRY, Dick	1956–57
CHERRY, Don	1954–55
CHERVYAKOV, Denis	1992–93
CHEVELDAE, Tim	1996–97
CHEVREFILS, Real	1951–52 - 1958–59
CHISHOLM, Art	1960–61
CHRISTIAN, Dave	1989–90 - 1990–91
CHURCH, Jack	1945–46
CHYNOWETH, Dean	1995–96 - 1997–98
CIMETTA, Robert	1988–89 - 1989–90
CLAPPER, Aubrey	1927–28 - 1946–47
CLARK, Andrew	1927–28
CLARK, Gordie	1974–75 - 1975–76
CLEGHORN, Sprague	1925–26 - 1927–28
COLVIN, Les	1948–49
CONACHER, Roy	1938–39 - 1941–42; 1945–46
CONNELLY, Wayne	1961–62 - 1963–64; 1966–67
CONNOR, Harry	1927–28; 1929–30
COOK, Alex	1931–32
COOK, Fred	1936–37
COOK, Lloyd	1924–25
COOPER, Carson	1924–25 - 1926–27
CORCORAN, Norm	1949–50; 1952–53; 1954–55
CORNFORTH, Mark	1995–96
COSTELLO, Murray	1954–55 - 1955–56
COTE, Alain	1985–86 - 1988–89

COURTEAU, Maurice	1943–44
COURTNALL, Geoff	1983–84 - 1987–88
COUTU, Billy	1926–27
COWLEY, Bill	1935–36 - 1946–47
CRAIG, Jim	1980–81
CRAWFORD, John	1937–38 - 1949–50
CRAWFORD, Lou	1989–90; 1991–92
CREIGHTON, Dave	1948–49 - 1953–54
CRISP, Terry	1965–66
CROWDER, Bruce	1981–82 - 1983–84
CROWDER, Keith	1980–81 - 1988–89
CUDE, Wilf	1931–32
CUPOLO, Bill	1944–45
CURRAN, Brian	1983–84 - 1985–86
CZERKAWSKI, Mariusz	1993–94 - 1995–96

D

DAFOE, Byron	1997–98
DAMORE, Nick	1941–42
DARRAGH, Hal	1930–31
DASKALAKIS, Cleon	1984–85 - 1986–87
DAVIE, Bob	1933–34 - 1935–36
DAVIS, Lorne	1955–56; 1959–60
DAVISON, Murray	1965–66
DEFELICE, Norm	1956–57
DelGUIDICE, Matt	1990–91
DELMONTE, Armand	1945–46
DeMARCO, Albert G.	1942–43 - 1943–44
DeMARCO, Albert T.	1978–79
DENNENY, Cy	1928–29
DERLAGO, Bill	1985–86
DILLABOUGH, Bob	1965–66 - 1966–67
DiMAIO, Rob	1996–97 - 1997–98
DOAK, Gary	1965–66 - 1969–70; 1972–73 - 1980–81
DOBBIN, Brian	1991–92
DONATELLI, Clark	1991–92
DONATO, Ted	1991–92 - 1997–98
DONNELLY, Dave	1983–84 - 1985–86
DORNHOEFER, Gary	1963–64 - 1965–66
DOURIS, Peter	1989–90 - 1992–93
DROVIN, P.C.	1996–97
DUFOUR, Luc	1982–83 - 1983–84
DUGUID, Lorne	1935–36 - 1936–37
DUMART, Woody	1935–36 - 1941–42; 1945–46 - 1953–54
DUNBAR, Dale	1988–89

E

EDESTRAND, Darryl	1973–74 - 1977–78
EGAN, Pat	1943–44 - 1948–49
EHMAN, Gerry	1957–58
ELIK, Todd	1995–96 - 1996–97
ELLETT, Dave	1997–98
EMMA, David	1996–97
EMMS, Leighton	1934–35
ERICKSON, Aut	1959–60 - 1960–61
ERICKSON, Grant	1968–69
ESPOSITO, Phil	1967–68 - 1975–76
EVANS, Claude	1957–58
EZINICKI, Bill	1950–51 - 1951–52

F

FEATHERSTONE, Glen	1991–92 - 1993–94
FERGUS, Tom	1981–82 - 1984–85
FERGUSON, Lorne	1949–50 - 1951–52; 1954–55 - 1955–56
FIELDER, Guyle	1953–54
FILLION, Marcel	1944–45
FILMORE, Tom	1933–34
FINNIGAN, Eddie	1935–36
FISHER, Duncan	1950–51 - 1952–53
FLAMAN, Ferny	1944–45 - 1950–51; 1954–55 - 1960–61

FLEMING, Reggie	1964–65 - 1965–66	
FLOCKHART, Ron	1988–89	
FORBES, Dave	1973–74 - 1976–77	
FORBES, Mike	1977–78	
FOSTER, Dwight	1977–78 - 1980–81; 1985–86 - 1986–87	
FOSTER, Harry	1931–32	
FOSTER, Norm	1990–91	
FOWLER, Norman	1924–25	
FRANKS, Jim	1943–44	
FREDERICKSON, Frank	1926–27 - 1928–29	
FROST, Harry	1938–39	

G

GAGNE, Art	1929–30
GAGNE, Pierre	1959–60
GAGNON, Johnny	1934–35
GAINOR, Norman	1927–28 - 1930–31
GALBRAITH, Percy	1926–27 - 1933–34
GALLEY, Gerry	1988–89 - 1991–92
GALLINGER, Don	1942–43 - 1943–44; 1945–46 - 1947–48
GAMBLE, Bruce	1960–61 - 1961–62
GARDINER, Bert	1943–44
GARDNER, Cal	1953–54 - 1956–57
GARIEPY, Ray	1953–54
GAUDREAULT, Armand	1944–45
GAUTHIER, Jean	1968–69
GELINEAU, Jack	1948–49 - 1950–51
GENDRON, Jean–Guy	1958–59 - 1960–61; 1962–63 - 1963–64
GERAN, George	1925–26
GETLIFFE, Ray	1935–36 - 1938–39
GIBBS, Barry	1967–68 - 1968–69
GIBSON, Doug	1973–74; 1975–76
GILBERT, Gilles	1973–74 - 1979–80
GILBERT, Jeannot	1962–63; 1964–65
GILL, Andre	1967–68
GILL, Hal	1997–98
GILLIS, Mike	1980–81 - 1983–84
GIROUX, Art	1934–35
GLADU, Paul	1944–45
GLENNON, Matt	1991–92
GODFREY, Warren	1952–53 - 1954–55; 1962–63
GOLDSWORTHY, Bill	1964–65 - 1966–67
GOLDSWORTHY, Roy	1936–37 - 1937–38
GORDON, Fred	1927–28
GORING, Butch	1984–85
GOULD, Bob	1989–90
GRACIE, Bob	1933–34
GRADIN, Thomas	1986–87
GRAHAM, Rod	1974–75
GRAHAM, Ted	1935–36
GRAHAME, Ron	1977–78
GRANT, Benny	1943–44
GRAY, Terry	1961–62
GREEN, Redvers	1928–29
GREEN, Ted	1960–61 - 1968–69; 1970–71 - 1971–72
GRONSDAHL, Lloyd	1941–42
GROSS, Lloyd	1933–34
GROSSO, Don	1946–47
GRUDEN, John	1993–94 - 1995–96
GRYP, Bob	1973–74
GUAY, Paul	1988–89
GUIDOLIN, Armand	1942–43 - 1943–44; 1945–46 - 1946–47

H

HAGMAN, Matti	1976–77 - 1977–78
HALL, Taylor	1987–88
HALWARD, Doug	1975–76 - 1977–78
HAMILL, Robert	1937–38 - 1941–42
HAMMOND, Ken	1990–91

HARKINS, Brett	1994–95; 1996–97
HARNOTT, Walter	1933–34
HARRINGTON, Leland	1925–26; 1927–28
HARRIS, Fred	1924–25; 1930–31
HARRISON, Ed	1947–48 - 1950–51
HARRISON, Jim	1968–69 - 1969–70
HAWGOOD, Gregg	1987–88–1989–90
HAYES, Chris	1971–72
HAYNES, Paul	1934–35
HEAD, Don	1961–62
HEADLEY, Fern	1924–25
HEBENTON, Andy	1963–64
HEINRICH, Lionel	1955–56
HEINZE, Steve	1991–92 - 1997–98
HENDERSON, John	1954–55 - 1955–56
HENDERSON, Murray	1944–45 - 1951–52
HENRY, Gordon	1948–49 - 1950–51; 1952–53
HENRY, Jim	1951–52 - 1954–55
HERBERTS, Jimmy	1924–25 - 1926–27
HERGESHEIMER, Phil	1941–42
HERVEY, Matt	1991–92
HEXIMER, Orville	1932–33
HICKS, Wayne	1962–63
HILL, Mel	1937–38 - 1940–41
HILLER, Wilbert	1941–42
HILLIER, Randy	1981–82 - 1983–84
HILLMAN, Floyd	1956–57
HILLMAN, Larry	1957–58 - 1959–60
HITCHMAN, Lionel	1924–25 - 1933–34
HODGE, Kenneth D.	1990–91 - 1991–92
HODGE, Kenneth R.	1967–68 - 1975–76
HODGSON, Ted	1966–67
HOLLETT, Bill	1935–36 - 1943–44
HOOVER, Ron	1989–90 - 1990–91
HORECK, Pete	1949–50 - 1950–51
HORVATH, Bronco	1957–58 - 1960–61
HOWE, Marty	1982–83
HUARD, Bill	1992–93
HUGHES, Brent	1991–92 - 1994–95
HUGHES, Ryan	1995–96
HURLEY, Paul	1968–69
HUSCROFT, Jamie	1993–94 - 1994–95
HUTTON, Bill	1929–30 - 1930–31
HYNES, Dave	1973–74 - 1974–75
HYNES, Gord	1991–92

I

IAFRATE, Al	1993–94
INGRAM, Jack	1924–25
IRVINE, Ted	1963–64

J

JACKSON, Art	1937–38; 1939–40 - 1944–45
JACKSON, Harvey	1941–42 - 1943–44
JACKSON, Percy	1931–32
JACKSON, Stan	1924–25 - 1925–26
JANNEY, Craig	1987–88 - 1991–92
JENKINS, Roger	1935–36
JENNINGS, Bill	1944–45
JEREMIAH, Ed	1932–33
JERWA, Frank	1931–32 - 1934–35
JERWA, Joe	1931–32; 1933–34; 1936–37
JOHNSON, Norm	1957–58
JOHNSON, Tom	1963–64 - 1964–65
JOHNSTON, Ed	1962–63 - 1972–73
JOHNSTON, Greg	1983–84 - 1989–90
JONATHAN, Stan	1975–76 - 1982–83
JONES, Ron	1971–72 - 1972–73
JOYCE, Bobby	1987–88 - 1989–90
JUNEAU, Joe	1991–92 - 1993–94
JUNKIN, Joe	1968–69

K

KALBFLEISH, Walt	1937–38

KAMINSKY, Max	1934–35 - 1935–36
KASATONOV, Alexei	1994–95 - 1995–96
KASPER, Steve	1980–81 - 1988–89
KEANS, Doug	1983–84 - 1987–88
KEENAN, Don	1958–59
KEKALAINEN, Jarmo	1989–90 - 1990–91
KENNEDY, Forbes	1962–63 - 1965–66
KENNEDY, Sheldon	1996–97
KHRISTICH, Dmitri	1997–98
KIMBLE, Darin	1992–93
KLEIN, Jim Lloyd	1928–29; 1931–32
KLUKAY, Joe	1952–53 - 1954–55
KLUZAK, Gord	1982–83 - 1990–91
KNIBBS, Bill	1964–65
KNIPSCHEER, Fred	1993–94 - 1994–95
KOPAK, Russ	1943–44
KOSTYNSKI, Doug	1983–84 - 1984–85
KRAFTCHECK, Steve	1950–51
KRAKE, Phil	1963–64; 1965–66 - 1967–68
KRUSHELNYSKI, Mike	1981–82 - 1983–84
KRYZANOWSKI, Ed	1948–49 - 1951–52
KULLMAN, Arnie	1947–48; 1949–50
KURTENBACH, Orland	1961–62; 1963–64 - 1964–65
KVARTALNOV, Dmitri	1992–93 - 1993–94
KYLE, Gus	1951–52

L

LaBINE, Leo	1951–52 - 1960–61
LABRIE, Guy	1943–44
LACHER, Blaine	1994–95 - 1995–96
LACROIX, Daniel	1994–95
LALONDE, Bobby	1979–80 - 1980–81
LAMB, Joe	1932–33 - 1933–34
LANE, Myles	1928–29 - 1929–30; 1933–34
LANG, Robert	1997–98
LANGDON, Steve	1974–75 - 1975–76; 1977–78
LANGLOIS, Al	1965–66
LAPOINTE, Guy	1983–84
LAROSE, Charles Bonner	1925–26
LAROSE, Guy	1994–95
LARSON, Reed	1985–86 - 1987–88
LAUDER, Martin	1927–28
LAVOIE, Dominic	1992–93
LAWTON, Brian	1989–90
LAYCOE, Hal	1950–51 - 1955–56
LAZARO, Jeff	1990–91 - 1991–92
LEACH, Larry	1958–59 - 1959–60; 1961–62
LEACH, Reg	1970–71 - 1971–72
LEACH, Steve	1991–92 - 1995–96
LEDUC, Richie	1972–73 - 1973–74
LEDYARD, Grant	1997–98
LEHMANN, Tommy	1987–88 - 1988–89
LEITER, Bob	1962–63 - 1965–66; 1968–69
LEMAY, Moe	1987–88 - 1988–89
LEMELIN, Reggie	1987–88 - 1992 - 93
LESUK, Bill	1968–69 - 1969–70
LESWICK, Pete	1944–45
LEVEILLE, Normand	1981–82 - 1982–83
LINSEMAN, Ken	1984–85 - 1989–90
LOCKHART, Howard	1924–25
LONSBERRY, Ross	1966–67 - 1968–69
LORENTZ, Jim	1968–69 - 1969–70
LOWE, Ross	1949–50 - 1950–51
LUKOWICH, Morris	1984–85 - 1985–86
LUMLEY, Harry	1957–58 - 1959–60
LUND, Pentti	1946–47 - 1947–48; 1951–52 - 1952–53
LYNN, Vic	1950–51 - 1951–52
LYONS, Peaches	1930–31

M

MacDONALD, Parker	1965–66
MacKAY, Mickey	1928–29 - 1929–30

MACKELL, Fleming	1951–52 - 1959–60
MacTAVISH, Craig	1979–80 - 1983–84
MAKELA, Mikko	1994–95
MALKOC, Dean	1996–97 - 1997–98
MALLETTE, Troy	1996–97
MALONEY, Phil	1949–50 - 1950–51
MALUTA, Ray	1975–76 - 1976–77
MANN, Cameron	1997–98
MANSON, Ray	1947–48
MANTHA, Sylvio	1936–37
MARCOTTE, Don	1965–66; 1968–69 - 1981–82
MARIO, Frank	1941–42; 1944–45
MARKWART, Nevin	1983–84 - 1987–88; 1989–90 - 1991–92
MAROIS, Daniel	1993–94
MAROTTE, Gilles	1965–66 - 1966–67
MARQUESS, Mark	1946–47
MARTIN, Clare	1941–42; 1946–47 - 1947–48
MARTIN, Frank	1952–53 - 1953–54
MARTIN, Hubert	1965–66 - 1966–67
MATTE, Joe	1925–26
MAXNER, Wayne	1964–65 - 1965–66
MAY, Alan	1987–88
McATEE, Norm	1946–47
McCARTHY, Tom	1960–61
McCARTHY, Tom J.	1986–87 - 1987–88
McCLEARY, Trent	1996–97
McCORD, Bob	1963–64 - 1964–65
McCREAVY, Pat	1938–39 - 1941–42
McCRIMMON, Brad	1979–80 - 1981–82
McDONALD, Alvin	1964–65
McEACHERN, Shawn	1995–96
McGILL, Jack	1941–42; 1944–45 - 1946–47
McINENLY, Bert	1933–34 - 1935–36
McINTYRE, Jack	1949–50 - 1952–53
McKECHNIE, Walt	1974–75
McKENNEY, Don	1954–55 - 1962–63
McKENZIE, John	1965–66 - 1971–72
McKIM, Andrew	1992–93 - 1993–94
McLAREN, Kyle	1995–96 - 1997–98
McLELLAN, Scott	1982–83
McMAHON, Mike	1945–46
McMANUS, Sammy	1936–37
McNAB, Peter	1976–77 - 1983–84
MEEKING, Harry	1926–27
MEISSNER, Dick	1959–60 - 1961–62
MELNYK, Larry	1980–81 - 1982–83
MICKOSKI, Nick	1959–60
MIDDLETON, Rick	1976–77 - 1987–88
MILBURY, Mike	1975–76 - 1986–87
MILLAR, Al	1957–58
MILLAR, Mike	1989–90
MILLER, Bob	1977–78 - 1980–81
MILLER, Jay	1985–86 - 1988–89
MITCHELL, Herb	1924–25 - 1925–26
MOFFAT, Mike	1981–82 - 1983–84
MOGER, Sandy	1994–95 - 1996–97
MOHNS, Doug	1953–54 - 1963–64
MOKOSAK, Carl	1988–89
MOOG, Andy	1987–88 - 1992–93
MORRIS, Bernie	1924–25
MORRIS, Jon	1993–94
MORRISON, Doug	1979–80 - 1981–82; 1984–85
MOTTER, Alex	1934–35 - 1935–36
MULLEN, Joe	1995–96
MURPHY, Gord	1991–92 - 1992–93
MURPHY, Ron	1965–66 - 1969–70
MURRAY, Glen	1991–92 - 1994–95
MYRVOLD, Anders	1996–97
N	
NASLUND, Mats	1994–95

NEELY, Cam	1986–87 - 1995–96
NEUFELD, Ray	1988–89 - 1989–90
NICHOLSON, Al	1955–56 - 1956–57
NICOLSON, Graeme	1978–79
NIELSEN, Kirk	1997–98
NIENHUIS, Kraig	1985–86 - 1987–88
NILAN, Chris	1990–91 - 1991–92
NILL, Jim	1983–84 - 1984–85
NORRIS, Jack	1964–65
NOWAK, Hank	1974–75–1976–77
O	
OATES, Adam	1991–92 - 1996–97
O'BRIEN, Dennis	1977–78 - 1979–80
O'BRIEN, Ellard	1955–56
O'CONNELL, Mike	1980–81 - 1985–86
ODDLEIFSON, Chris	1972–73 - 1973–74
ODGERS, Jeff	1996–97
O'DONNELL, Fred	1972–73 - 1983–84
O'DWYER, Billy	1987–88 - 1989–90
OLIVER, Harry	1926–27 - 1933–34
OLIVER, Murray	1960–61 - 1966–67
O'NEIL, James	1933–34 - 1936–37
O'NEIL, Paul	1975–76
O'REE, Willie	1957–58; 1960–61
O'REILLY, Terry	1971–72 - 1984–85
ORR, Bobby	1966–67 - 1975–76
OUELLETTE, Gerry	1960–61
OWEN, George	1928–29 - 1932–33
P	
PACHAL, Clayton	1976–77 - 1977–78
PALLAZZARI, Al	1943–44
PALMER, Brad	1982–83
PANAGABKO, Ed	1955–56 - 1956–57
PANTELEEV, Grigori	1992–93 - 1994–95
PARENT, Bernie	1965–66 - 1966–67
PARISE, Jean–Paul	1965–66 - 1966–67
PARK, Brad	1975–76 - 1982–83
PASIN, Dave	1985–86
PATTERSON, George	1933–34
PAYNE, Davis	1995–96 - 1996–97
PEDERSEN, Allen	1986–87 - 1990–91
PEDERSON, Barry	1980–81 - 1985–86
PEETERS, Pete	1982–83 - 1985–86
PEIRSON, John	1946–47 - 1953–54; 1955–56 - 1957–58
PENNINGTON, Cliff	1961–62 - 1962–63
PERREAULT, Bob	1962–63
PETERS, Garry	1971–72
PETERS, Jimmy	1947–48 - 1948–49
PETTIE, Jim	1976–77 - 1978–79
PETTINGER, Eric	1928–29
PETTINGER, Gordon	1937–38 - 1939–40
PIDHIRNY, Harry	1957–58
PLANTE, Jacques	1972–73
PLETT, Willi	1987–88
PODLOSKI, Ray	1988–89
POILE, Norman	1949–50
POLIZIANI, Dan	1958–59
POPIEL, Paul	1965–66
PORTLAND, Jack	1934–35 - 1939–40
POTVIN, Marc	1994–95 - 1995–96
POULIN, Dave	1989–90 - 1992–93
PRAJSLER, Peter	1991–92
PRATT, Jack	1930–31 - 1931–32
PRATT, Walter	1946–47
PRENTICE, Dean	1962–63 - 1965–66
PRONOVOST, Andre	1960–61 - 1962–63
PRONOVOST, Claude	1955–56
PROPP, Brian	1989–90
PRPIC, Joel	1997–98
PUSIE, Jean	1934–35

Q	
QUACKENBUSH, Bill	1949–50 - 1955–56
QUACKENBUSH, Max	1950–51
QUILTY, John	1947–78
QUINTAL, Stephane	1988–89 - 1991–92
R	
RANFORD, Bill	1985–86 - 1986–87; 1995–96 - 1996–97
RANIERI, George	1956–57
RATELLE, Jean	1975–76 - 1980–81
RATHWELL, Jack	1974–75
RAVLICH, Matt	1962–63; 1971–72 - 1972–73
REARDON, Terry	1938–39 - 1940–41; 1945–46 - 1946–47
REDAHL, Gordon	1958–59
REDDING, George	1924–25 - 1925–26
REDMOND, Dick	1978–79 - 1981–82
REECE, Dave	1975–76
REGAN, Larry	1956–57 - 1958–59
REIBEL, Earl	1958–59
REID, Dave	1983–84 - 1987–88; 1991–92 - 1995–96
REIGLE, Ed	1950–51
RICHER, Stephane	1992–93
RICHTER, Barry	1996–97
RIENDEAU, Vincent	1993–94 - 1994–95
RIGGIN, Pat	1958–56 - 1986–87
RILEY, Jack	1935–36
RING, Bobby	1965–66
RIPLEY, Vic	1932–33 - 1933–34
RITTINGER, Alan	1943–44
RIVERS, Wayne	1963–64 - 1966–67
ROBERTS, Doug	1971–72 - 1973–74
ROBERTS, Gord	1992–93 - 1993–94
ROBERTS, Maurice	1925–26
ROBITAILLE, Randy	1996–97 - 1997–98
ROCHE, Earl	1932–33
RODDEN, Eddie	1928–29
ROHLOFF, Jon	1994–95 - 1996–97
ROLFE, Dale	1959–60
ROMANO, Roberto	1986–87
RONTY, Paul	1947–48 - 1950–51
ROWE, Bobby	1924–25
ROY, Andre	1995–96 - 1996–97
ROY, Jean–Yves	1996–97 - 1997–98
ROZZINI, Gino	1944–45
RUHNKE, Kent	1975–76
RUNGE, Paul	1930–31 - 1931–32; 1935–36
RUZICKA, Vladimir	1990–91 - 1992–93
S	
SAMSONOV, Sergei	1997–98
SANDERSON, Derek	1965–66 - 1973–74
SANDFORD, Ed	1947–48 - 1954–55
SANDS, Charlie	1934–35 - 1938–39
SARNER, Craig	1974–75
SATHER, Glen	1966–67 - 1968–69
SAVAGE, Gordon	1934–35
SAVARD, Andre	1973–74 - 1975–76
SAWCHUK, Terry	1955–56 - 1956–57
SAWYER, Kevin	1995–96 - 1996–97
SCHAFER, Paxton	1996–97
SCHERZA, Charlie	1943–44
SCHMAUTZ, Bob	1973–74 - 1979–80
SCHMIDT, Clarence	1943–44
SCHMIDT, John	1942–43
SCHMIDT, Joseph	1943–44
SCHMIDT, Milt	1936–37 - 1941–42; 1945–46 - 1954–55
SCHNARR, Werner	1924–25 - 1925–26
SCHOCK, Danny	1969–70 - 1970–71
SCHOCK, Ron	1963–64 - 1966–67

SCHOENFELD, Jim	1983–84		
SECORD, Al	1978–79 - 1980–81	**T**	
SEROWIK, Jeff	1994–95	TALLAS, Rob	1995–96 - 1997–98
SHACK, Ed	1967–68 - 1968–69	TATARINOV, Mikhail	1993–94
SHALDYBIN, Yevgeny	1996–97	TAYLOR, Billy	1947–48
SHANAHAN, Sean	1977–78	TAYLOR, Bobby	1929–30
SHANNON, Gerry	1934–35 - 1935–36	TAYLOR, Tim	1997–98
SHAW, David	1992–93 - 1994–95	TEAL, Allen	1954–55
SHAY, Normie	1924–25 - 1925–26	TESSIER, Orval	1955–56; 1960–61
SHEPHARD, John	1933–34	THELIN, Mats	1984–85 - 1986–87
SHEPPARD, Gregg	1972–73 - 1977–78	THELVEN, Michael	1985–86 - 1986–87
SHEWCHUK, Jack	1938–39 - 1942–43; 1944–45	THOMLINSON, Dave	1991–92
SHIELDS, Allen	1936–37	THOMPSON, Cecil	1928–29 - 1938–39
SHILL, Bill	1942–43; 1945–46 - 1946–47	THOMPSON, Cliff	1941–42; 1948–49
SHILL, Jack	1934–35	THOMS, Bill	1944–45
SHOEBOTTOM, Bruce	1987–88 - 1990–91	THORNTON, Joe	1997–98
SHORE, Eddie	1926–27 - 1939–40	TIMANDER, Mattias	1996–97 - 1997–98
SIEBERT, Albert	1933–34 - 1935–36	TOCCHET, Rick	1995–96 - 1996–97
SILK, Dave	1983–84 - 1984–85	TOPPAZZINI, Jerry	1952–53 - 1953–54; 1955–56 -
SIMMER, Charlie	1984–85 - 1986–87		1963–64
SIMMONS, Al	1973–74; 1975–76	TOPPAZZINI, Zellio	1948–49 - 1950–51
SIMMONS, Don	1956–57 - 1960–61	TOWNSHEND, Graeme	1989–90 - 1990–91
SIMONETTI, Frank	1983–84 - 1987–88	TUOHEY, George	1931–32
SIMS, Al	1973–74 - 1978–79	TURLIK, Gordon	1959–60
SKINNER, Alfie	1924–25	**V**	
SKRIKO, Petri	1990–91 - 1991–92	VACHON, Rogie	1980–81 - 1981–82
SLEIGHER, Louis	1984–85 - 1985–86	VADNAIS, Carol	1971–72 - 1975–76
SMILLIE, Don	1933–34	VAN IMPE, Darren	1997–98
SMITH, Alex	1932–33 - 1933–34	VESEY, Jim	1991–92
SMITH, Barry	1975–76	VON STEFENELLI, Phillip	1995–96
SMITH, Dallas	1959–60 - 1961–62; 1965–66 -	**W**	
	1976–77	WALTON, Mike	1970–71 - 1972–73; 1978–79
SMITH, Des	1939–40 - 1941–42	WALZ, Wes	1989–90 - 1990–91
SMITH, Floyd	1954–55; 1956–57	WARD, Don	1959–60
SMITH, Ken	1944–45 - 1950–51	WARWICK, Grant	1947–48 - 1948–49
SMITH, Reginald	1936–37	WATSON, Joe	1964–65; 1966–67
SMITH, Rick	1968–69 - 1971–72; 1976–77 -	WEBSTER, Tom	1968–69 - 1969–70
	1979–80	WEILAND, Ralph	1928–29 - 1931–32; 1935–36 -
SMOLINSKI, Bryan	1992–93 - 1994–95		1938–39
SONGIN, Tom	1978–79 - 1980–81	WENSINK, John	1976–77 - 1979–80
SPARROW, Emory	1924–25	WESLEY, Glen	1987–88 - 1993–94
SPEER, Bill	1969–70 - 1970–71	WESTFALL, Ed	1961–62 - 1971–72
SPENCER, Irvin	1962–63	WIEMER, Jim	1989–90 - 1993–94
SPRING, Frank	1969–70	WILCOX, Archie	1933–34
STAIOS, Steve	1995–96 - 1996–97	WILKINS, Barry	1966–67; 1968–69 - 1969–70
STANFIELD, Fred	1967–68 - 1972–73	WILKINSON, Jack	1943–44
STANLEY, Allan	1956–57 - 1957–58	WILLIAMS, Burr	1934–35
STANTON, Paul	1993–94	WILLIAMS, Tom	1961–62 - 1968–69
STAPLETON, Pat	1961–62 - 1962–63	WILSON, Gordie	1954–55
STASIUK, Vic	1955–56 - 1960–61		
STEVENS, Kevin	1995–96	WILSON, Landon	1996–97 - 1997–98
STEVENS, Mike	1987–88	WILSON, Ross	1957–58
STEVENS, Phil	1925–26	WILSON, Wally	1947–48
STEVENSON, Shayne	1990–91 - 1991–92	WINKLER, Hal	1926–27 - 1927–28
STEWART, Al	1991–92	WINNES, Chris	1990–91 - 1992–93
STEWART, Bob	1971–72	WISEMAN, Ed	1939–40 - 1941–42
STEWART, Cam	1993–94 - 1996–97	WOYTOWICH, Bob	1964–65 - 1966–67
STEWART, Charles	1924–25 - 1926–27	**Y**	
STEWART, Jim	1979–80	YACKEL, Ken	1958–59
STEWART, Nels	1932–33 - 1934–35; 1936–37	YOUNG, C.J.	1992–93
STEWART, Ron	1965–66 - 1966–67	**Z**	
STUART, Billy	1924–25 - 1926–27	ZANUSSI, Joe	1975–76 - 1976–77
STUMPEL, Jozef	1991–92 - 1996–97	ZHOLTOK, Sergei	1992–93 - 1993–94
SULLIVAN, George	1949–50 - 1952–53	ZOMBO, Rick	1995–96
SULLIVAN, Mike	1997–98		
SUTHERLAND, Ron	1931–32		
SUTTER, Ron	1995–96		
SWEENEY, Bob	1986–87 - 1991–92		
SWEENEY, Don	1988–89 - 1997–98		
SWEENEY, Tim	1992–93; 1995–96 - 1996–97		
SYLVESTRI, Don	1984–85		

PHOTOGRAPHY CREDITS